Ecstatic Pudding

– JOY RICE –

An environmentally friendly book printed and bound in England by
www.printondemand-worldwide.com

Mixed Sources
Product group from well-managed
forests, and other controlled sources
www.fsc.org Cert no. TT-COC-002641
© 1996 Forest Stewardship Council

PEFC Certified
This product is
from sustainably
managed forests
and controlled
sources

www.pefc.org

PEFC/16-33-415

This book is made entirely of chain-of-custody materials

www.fast-print.net/store.php

ECSTATIC PUDDING
Copyright © Joy Rice 2014

A catalogue record for this book is available from the British Library

ISBN 978-178456-079-9

First published 2014 by
FASTPRINT PUBLISHING
Peterborough, England.

Ecstatic pudding

by Joy Rice

Dedicated to my family -

Denis, Adam, Edwin and Heather, Abbigail and Oliver.
The inspiration for some of my poems!

1 The reason why I write rubbish poems

Whenever there's a special occasion,
or something to celebrate.
I like to compose a poem…
…something that my children hate!

One thinks that my poems are silly.
Another calls them crap,
and the middle one would really,
prefer it if I didn't try to rap!

But, I like to put pen to paper,
or finger to computer key,
to express those special feelings,
of how much they mean to me.

So, family, you'll just have to put up with it,
each time there's a special event or date,
because you'll probably get a poem from me,
to help you celebrate!

Contents

Women's problems

Life

Ecstatic Pudding

A bit about me and why I write...

I can vaguely remember learning to write. Hours of handwriting practice at School looping swirls with bits that had to go above the line and tails that had to go below. I never did get a perfect handwriting script. Now, thank goodness for computers, my writing is perfect...ish!

However, I did like writing. My ambition at 10 was to be an authoress. I never did get there either! As an adult I joined a creative writing class in the 90's, which I enjoyed but still no novel, no blockbuster book...but a curious knack of writing humorous verse.
Momentum for writers – mo_mentum@btinternet.com
Thanks to Mo, my teacher, who gave me lots of encouragement!

I did discover a 'gift' (if you can call it that!) of being able to put together a poem. Some may call it doggerel, or worse, but I am encouraged by the fact that people seem to enjoy my poems and ask for copies.

So, my ambition now as an 'adult'...is to go viral as an internet and published poet! Hope you enjoy these poems! Please note the numbers are for the poems – not the pages.

Ecstatic pudding - This chapter is just that - poems about me, odd things that have happened to me or just my thoughts.

All are true! Especially – "The Perfect Nurse's Hat" - I really did go out on Vernon Park with a sanitary towel on my head. (Oops I've spoilt the poem now!)

2   Ecstatic pudding

Sometimes people get my name wrong.
So here - let me be emphatic.
It's Rice as in pudding.
And Joy as in ecstatic!

3   Ambition

I have a burning ambition,
  to become a household name.
I crave adulation,
  and I want instant fame.

I want to be a household name ,
  talked about each and every day,
and I want to be a 'fly on the wall',
  just to hear what people say.

Maybe – "that Joy Rice is brilliant;
  her literary works are ace,
She's got a terrific figure,
  and a drop-dead gorgeous face".

My opinions would be sought after,
governments would clamour for me.
I'd entertain the Prime Minister,
  and invite the Queen to tea.

The press would seek me out,
for I'd be a news-worthy item.
They'd better not put me on page 3,
or else I'd threaten to bite 'em!

I'd be the darling of the press;
the paparazzi would be my friend.
Everyone would follow my lead,
 and my poems would start a new trend.

My Tweets and Facebook comments,
would create an internet spiral.
And wait 'till you see my YouTube clips,
they would be going viral!

I'd like my fifteen minutes of fame,
to last for at least an hour.
I'd take over all the TV channels ,
(now that would be real power!)

I don't suppose this will happen to me,
despite all my plans and schemes.
But it's good to have an ambition,
I guess, even if it's all in my dreams.

4   Earthquake

Lying in my Ikea bed,
snuggled up next to my spouse,
drifting off into dreamland,
when something bloody BIG shook and shook the house!

It was early Wednesday morning,
February 27th 2008,
as I lay snug as a bug in bed,
next to my lifetime mate.

Only thirty minutes earlier,
as I'd got into bed,
'im indoors snuggled up to me
"How about it?" he'd sexily said.

Well, I'd had a busy morning,
a busy afternoon and busy evening too.
So I gave him a kiss said "Sorry mi'duck,
tomorrow will have to do".

And then at zero zero fifty five a.m.
the night still as black as pitch.
I was awakened from my slumbers,
as our entwined limbs began to twitch.

I thought that he'd had a seizure,
a weird fit or maybe a stroke.
Cos let's face it, he's not getting any younger,
in fact he's becoming a real old bloke!

Then as suddenly as the trembles had started;
they very quickly stopped.
I was wide awake now,
as out of the bed the 'stroke victim' hopped.

My daughter appeared on the landing,
Saying "what the f@*& was that?"
My son joined in the fracas.
The only one unperturbed was the cat!

I thought the shake was a tremor.
Hubby thought it was a sinking mine shaft.
My daughter thought it was an earth-hurtling satellite.
My son thought we were all daft!

The morning news informed us,
we'd had an earthquake - 5.3 on the Richter scale.
We'd all had a seismic experience
and lived to tell the tale!

But how different it could have been,
if I'd responded to his earlier overtures to love-making.
We could have been at the heights of passion,
when the whole of the midlands was shaking!

And then we would have truly known,
that our ardour and love was ever true,
and I could have asked him in all honestly
"Well, did I make the earth move for you?"

So the moral of this poem is-

Never turn down an offer,
of a dalliance with your male.
Earthquakes only happen rarely,
and it's your chance to hit the Richter scale!

5   <u>Epitaph</u>

She made it her mission in life.
To be irritating and to annoy.
Some people called her a miserable old bag,
whilst others simply called her Joy.

A hundred lovers stood weeping,
at her graveside, clutching red roses.
The tears trickled down their faces,
and ran off the end of their noses.

Her family and friends were beside themselves,
They were all in disarray.
Whatever would they do now...
...that their Joy had gone away?

But, Joy left them a message,
to cheer them on their way.
The minister read it out,
and this is what it did say...

Don't be sad.
Don't be despaired.
For I'm not dead.
I'm life impaired.

When I am dead and gone from here.
Don't cry for me, don't shed a tear.
For, I have had a happy life, achieved the goals I'd planned.
Now, I am going to walk with Him and He will take my hand.

I've green pastures to be led by,
and quiet waters to dip my toes.
There's a party waiting for me,
 and my cup overflows.

On earth the only mansion,
that I knew was a polish spray.
But in heaven, there's a real one,
 waiting for me to live in ...someday.

I'm not too keen on actually dying,
I hope that it doesn't hurt much.
I hope that I'll slip off in my sleep...
...awaiting Jesus' gentle touch.

And then all my aches and pains,
will be gone in the blink of His eye.
The angels will be rejoicing in Heaven.
Hallelujahing on the day that I die.

My faulty frail human body,
 will be stripped of its earthly veneer.
And I shall be a free spirit,
with death as a whole new career!

I shall be at His left hand in Heaven,
 (the right place has already gone).
And I will be there with my Saviour,
 for all of eternity long.

So, please do not sob or be sorry,
don't grieve for me when I leave.
For, I know that I shall be in paradise;
 yes that's what I truly believe.

7   Fifty

How are you supposed to behave at fifty?
I'm really not too sure.
I've been lots of other significant ages,
but, I've never been fifty before.

On the inside I still feel quite young.
On the outside, I no longer look like me!
My body still works fairly reasonably,
but, perhaps not quite as it used to be.

Sometimes, I feel as though I'm only thirty,
with bags of energy all of the time!
Other times, I feel like something the cat's thrown up,
and then I know that I'm no longer forty-nine.

I've still got all of my own teeth,
and most of my faculties too!
There's not too much grey in my hair,
and wrinkles - well there's only a few.

There's a lot that can be done with plastic surgery,
but I'm too stingy to pay out loads of money.
And any, implants, tummy tucks and Botox,
can make you look downright funny!

I'm still having 'the visitors' each month time.
I think that you'll know what I mean.
That's something I'll be glad to see the end of,
as they've been visiting since I was thirteen.

So, what does the future hold for me?
The menopause, old age and death.
Well, I'd better enjoy life while I've got it.
As long as I can still draw breath.

But hold on a minute... what's fifty?
Half of a century - only a mere five decades.
There's plenty of life that I can enjoy still.
and I shall enjoy it in spades!

There are places that I plan to visit.
A whole wide world to explore,
and now there are no children to take with me,
then I can afford to go away more!

I can wear any fashion I fancy (within reason).
I can have a tattoo or dye my hair.
I don't have to worry about what other people think,
I can do what I like without any care.

So, long live being fifty that's what I say.
You're as old as you feel - it's true!
A positive outlook, a low-fat diet
And I can feel like I'm only forty-two!

8   Horror of horrors!

I want to be a writer, and would give almost anything,
to be able to write best sellers just like Stephen King.
But, when I put my pen to paper,
my brain goes funny and my thoughts start to caper.
My writing catches me unawares,
'cause instead of Stephen King ... I write like Pam Ayres!

9   I may not be your cup of tea

I may not be your cup of tea,
but I might just be your cappuccino.
I may not be the works of Shakespeare,
but I might be a much loved Beano.

I may not be the flavour of the month.
I might not ring your bell.
I may set your teeth on edge.
It might be that we just don't gel.

You may think that I'm a pain in the neck.
Or I might be a thorn in your side.
It may be that I can never please you...
...No matter how hard I've tried!

So...I may not be your cup of tea.
PG tips? Herbal? Earl Grey or decaf?
I may not be to your taste...
...but I'm always good for a laugh.

When I look at the back of my hands,
I can see age spots aplenty.
An unsightly clue to my aging,
that wasn't there when I was twenty!

I catch a glimpse of my reflection,
and see the thing that I dread.
My flat once size 10 stomach,
has turned into middle age spread.

Where once my hair was golden,
it's now got silver streaks.
And jobs that I could do in hours,
I put off now for weeks.

I struggle to kneel down to garden.
My knees are giving me jip,
and sometimes when I'm out walking,
I get a pain in my right hip.

The print in books and newspapers,
is getting to be far too small to read.
And supermarkets are so confusing,
I cannot find the goods that I need.

The sound on my TV and radio,
is getting soft and muffled.
I seem to have forgotten how to multi-task,
I often get kerfuffled!

But looking on the plus side.
I've outlived my old Mum and Dad.
And I still have all my own teeth.
So - things cannot be all bad!

I can get dressed up in any outfit.
I no longer care what people think.
I no longer have to prove what my age is,
when purchasing alcoholic drink.

It's time to take a rest from working.
Time to spend some time on 'me'.
Too young to qualify as retired,
so, I'm just going to be job-free!

11   Joy by name...Joy by nature

It's hard to be pleasant and happy all the time,
I'm sure that you will agree.
But, it's especially difficult and challenging,
when you have a name like me.

It really is a problem when you're christened,
with a name like mine ...that is Joy.
People have expectations of you...
...such as Joy's should be nice and not annoy!

People say tritely, "Joy by name,
and Joy by nature".
But, when they find out you're not a 'Joy',
then they start to hate yer.

Joys are supposed to be happy,
with a sunny disposition.
Well, I can tell you, pal,
that's a wrong supposition.

Joys can be nasty,
and as angry as can be.
Joys are heavily into,
making people suffer from their PMT.

Joys are never wrong.
Joys are always right.
So you better watch out,
'cause some Joys also bite!

So, when you meet me,
and I'm introduced as Joy.
You better treat me with respect,
"cause I'm no hoi polloi!

Then you'll find out in time,
things will turn out great,
and I'll eventually be,
your greatest Joy-full mate!

12   Misplaced snowflake

Whilst stepping out in Bulwell.
I really didn't think twice.
I put my best foot forward,
and slipped on some invisible ice.

I felt myself flipping - in slow motion
I didn't understand what I'd done.
There was nothing for me to hold on to,
so I landed on my bum.

This tale of woe goes on for ever.
I'm sure that you will agree.
It's best that I shorten the story.
Needless to say, I ended up at the QMC!

Now I'm known for embroidering my stories
But, I don't want you to think that I'd fib ya...
...For I really had breaks in three places.
One in the Fib' and two in the Tibia.

It takes time to repair broken bones.
The consultant says "at least 16 weeks.
Get cracking on the crutches,
you'll have to learn new mobility techniques!"

So, I'm at home, having a rest with my feet up.
Or as some people would say 'having a break'.
I'm hibernating this winter and spring,
all because of a misplaced snowflake.

Was it just to miss this winter season?

This time spent at home has been restful.
Time to reflect, read, think, ponder and pray.
And the next time it snows here in Bulwell,
I shall only go out in a sleigh!

Moral
Take my advice.
You better think twice.
Snow can be nice...
but watch out for the ice!

Written whilst recuperating from my broken leg!

My mother was a canny old soul,
with much wisdom to impart.
Her best advice she'd give to me,
from the bottom of her heart.
When I was a little girl, much smaller than today,
she took me to one side and this is what she did say.

Whatever you do.
Wherever you go.
However you live your life.
Take this tip from me,
and I'll guarantee
you'll save yourself lots of strife.

The men you'll meet will be many,
like pebbles on the sand.
You can take your pick,
so don't need to be quick.
Before you let one have your hand.

You'll meet men sincere.
You'll meet men that are queer.
You'll meet men that are pretty weird.
But...whatever you do,
your whole life through...
...don't marry a man with a beard!

For a beard can be prickly and tickly and tough,
with bristles that scratch you and make your skin rough.
A beard harbours a haven to an invisible host...
...of creepies and crawlies - he'll have the most!

You may think that he's cute, when he is in pursuit,
But, daughter, beware of the man that's hirsute.
Oh daughter, watch out, you are heading for trouble,
when you fall for a man with designer stubble.
For a man with a beard has got something to hide.
He'll tell you that he wears it to show off his macho pride.

But, under that face that is all wiry,
lurks a passionate man with a soul all fiery.
So, watch what you do with a man with a whisker,
'cause all he wants to do is to ravish and frisk yer.

I pondered Mums' words on my journey through life.
As I considered each man and my role as a wife.
Did I take mothers advice? I hear you query.
Did I hell? I chose a man all passionate and hairy!

14   Mum

My mum would be spinning in her grave,
except that we had her cremated,
if she knew the price that I pay today,
for goods that she'd consider over-rated.

Just the other day as I was spreading my bread,
with my pro-biotic, bio-organic cholesterol, low-fat spread,
I could imagine my mother having a chunter and a mutter,
to see me eating posh, expensive marg, instead of good
old -fashioned butter.

And marg priced at nearly three quid a tub!
She'd never believe that I could ever afford,
to buy margarine that costs as much...
...as I used to pay her, begrudgingly, for my board.

Mum would be amazed at the food I purchase.
Exotic fruit and veg that was beyond her means.
But at least she'd be thankful,
that at long last I've started eating 'my greens'.

And Kiwi fruit - now what is on earth is that?
"Looks like something that's been hacked up by the cat".
In her day, Kiwi just hadn't been invented.
An apple a day kept her happy and contented.

Yes, good old fashioned food was in,
like spotted dick or finnan haddock.
And if mum wanted any cookery tips,
well it was the Be-ro book or Fanny Craddock.

Now, it's wall to wall television cooks,
whenever you put on the telly,
showing off their posh puds like Tiramisu,
instead of mum's signature dish of chopped bananas and lime
jelly.

Well, now Mum's gone where there's no cooking anymore,
no supermarkets, shops, markets or merchandise.
No washing up, no cleaning, no chasing after me.
Yes, she's truly gone to her reward in Paradise!

15   My Mum

Now, don't get me started on about TV,
'cause Mum only had black and white.
Colour was for folk with more money than sense.
People who never could look after the pounds and the pence.

Washing was done in a dolly tub,
with a block of hard green soap.
An automatic washer dryer like I have now,
Mum would never have dared to hope.

And beating carpets with a broom handle,
was the best way to get them clean.
Fitted carpets although too pricy,
was every housewife's dream.   .

But, now I've had my fitted carpets taken out.
What a shock that'd be for my old mum!
As she'd be amazed at my laminated floor,
and proclaim "it's just like linoleum!"

16   <u>Night time thoughts</u>

I keep a pen and notebook ready,
In a drawer beside my bed.
So, that I can jot down my musings,
as they pop into my head.

So, if my thoughts be shallow,
or at rare times they be deep.
It's just the stuff my brain clears out,
as I drop off to sleep.

It's just as well really,
that my mind discards these schemes.
For, goodness knows what I'd be doing,
If they all stayed in my dreams!

17   Poem a day

Do you think that it would be possible?
For me to write a poem a day?
I suppose I could try to do it.
But, would I run out of things to say?

I like to put words together.
I like to make my poems rhyme.
I could try to challenge myself to do this.
But can I really spare the time?

It could be a kind of poetic diary.
A record of events and stuff.
No, I don't think I could really be bothered.
I've already had enough!

In future years when I'm no longer here.
 Will you read my poems and think,
my goodness what a load of £%$&,
she must have written these when she'd had a drink?

Poem a week

I try to write a poem a week.
Some weeks I can manage even more.
There was a time when my brain was younger,
when I actually managed four!

Some days I just write a verse,
other days a witty line.
Some days I struggle for ages,
because I cannot find the perfect rhyme.

I've that heard writing poetry is therapeutic.
A creative craft, an artistic skill.
I think of poems as a way to organise my thoughts,
and if I can make it humorous, then even better still!

My poems are full of foibles.
True life with all its strange little quirks.
I like to record the oddities in my life.
Well that; just how my neurons are hot-wired.
That's how my brain works!

I keep a pen and a notebook, to hand all of the time.
So, that when I get the muse upon me,
I can get down that elusive rhyme.

I know that my poems often surprise people.
I'm used to my share of odd looks.
I suppose this rhyming streak I've got,
is being brought up on Rupert Bear books!

I'd love to write a great novel.
A classic, epic saga from my pen I'd dash.
Then I'd be immortalised in print forever,
and hopefully earn lots of cash!

19 Poets

Poets are only famous,
when they are dead and gone.
like Byron, Shelley and thingamajig...
... what's-his-name – that other one.

I don't think that there's money to be made as a poet.
Except when you've popped your clogs.
Because not many people are bothered,
about doggerel or rhyming monologues.

I'd love to be a published poet.
I think that would be a great wheeze.
I'd go off to literary functions,
and I'd get paid lots of royalty fees!

So, I guess I write these verses for fun.
But, wouldn't it be really great.
If somehow, I could be offered,
the job of Poet Laureate!

I try to be happy.
I try to be Merry.
I owe my poetry skills,
to my rhyming dictionary.

20 Possession

I think that I've been taken over!
I don't want to sound too brash.
But, since I've been writing poetry,
I think I'm possessed by Ogden Nash.

21   Rice & Wood

I suppose it's very flattering.
I suppose I ought to feel good.
That people often say to me,
"You're just like that Victoria Wood!"

I suppose it would be different.
I suppose it would be nice.
If people said to Victoria.
"You're just like that Joy Rice!"

22   Shortly

Please don't call me shortly!
It really messes with my head.
Please don't call me shortly!
It makes me see bright red!

I'm five feet and a half inch,
when in my stockinged feet.
I'm height enhanced – vertically challenged,
or as I'd prefer to say – petite!

Now, I might be getting touchy.
Perhaps it's because I'm a certain age.
But fifty odd years of being called shortly,
brings me out in a sizist rage.

"I'll be seeing you shortly",
is what people often say to me.
Please don't call me shortly!
It's really rankles with me!

When making phone calls,
 it happens time and time again.
Your call is important to us,
(it really is a pain).

I could manage with the waiting,
and the boring pan-pipe tune.
If instead of my call being dealt with shortly,
it could be dealt with soon!

I've even seen it on cash machines,
in letters glowing fluorescent green.
Your money will be available shortly.
Oh it makes me feel so mean!

So please consider what you call me.
I can be little – I can be brief.
I can be small – wish I was tall.
But shortly gives me so much grief!

23   Superhero

I'd like to be a superhero.
I'd be wonderwoman – there's no doubt!
I'd wear a costume that holds the wobbly bits in,
and pushes all the right bits out!

I'd zoom around doing good deeds.
I'd be the Prodigy of Piccadilly.
I'd be the Boadicea of Bulwell.
Even though my costume made me look silly.

I'd be busy righting wrongs.
I'd be fastly fighting crime.
I'd set up a Neighbourhood Watch.
I might even write a rhyme!

I've been a superhero before.
It's true – I even had special powers.
I used to be the Church secretary,
and could turn the elders' minutes into hours!

Once upon a long time when I was just a little girly,
and shared a bedroom with my older sister Shirley.

I was playing my favourite game of dressing up as a nurse,
but couldn't find my nurse's hat - Oh drat! Oh curse!

Then, I remembered Shirl had some special ones in a drawer.
A packet with lots in - I wondered what she had them for?

I tried one on - a perfect fit - with the loops around my ears,
and off I went playing dress-up - blissfully unawares.

I took my teddy for a pram ride, off for Vernon Park.
Happy as a nurse could be - oh what a jolly lark!

I never noticed people's stares, their sniggers and weird looks.
I was happy pushing teddy and going to see the ducks.

The trouble came when I got home and my mother became
manic!
She took one look at me and then began to panic.

Joy! You've never been out all day like that,
with that 'thing' on your head, instead of a hat!

Mum went ballistic, my sister Shirl laughed,
and I was sent to bed - not knowing why -
but feeling rather daft.

Many years passed and then I reached my teens.
Eventually the 'visitors' came - and you know what that
means!

Then I burnt up with shame, my face turned a crimson red,
as I realised that I'd been on Vernon Park with a sanitary towel
on my head!

A warning to you mothers - to your daughters be explanatory,
so they won't go off wearing headgear that's meant for
something sanitary!

My mistake was genuine I thought these hats would be alright.
For they were obviously medical as they were called Doctor
White!

25   There's a mansion up in Heaven

There's a mansion up in heaven,
that's promised, just for me.
It's full of all mod-cons,
with a view over the cloudy sea.

It's built in a classic style.
It has such elegant lines.
Better than any building ,
you will ever find on Grand Designs.

I'm not quite ready to take up residence.
I've too much living to do.
But, I can dream what it will be like ...
...and ponder for a moment or two.

So, when I get fed up with my lot,
with all its trouble and strife.
I can hope for better things to come...
... in Heaven...in my next life.

Religious stuff - Trying to be a good Christian

I always attended Sunday School as a child until teenage years when I found better things to do. I'll leave that to your imagination! Returning to Church as an adult and being baptised in 1980, I have always tried to be a good person. But, perhaps not always a good Christian!

I have a fridge magnet that says –

If you can't be a good example – then be a terrible warning.

So, I guess I am the terrible warning!
Hope you find some fun, as well as something to make you think, in these poems

26   <u>5+2 = loads!</u>

The boy went to see the preacher, and he sort of had a hunch, that maybe it would be a good idea to take a picnic lunch.

Five loaves and two fishes. Yum – a tasty picnic snack!
He'll listen to the preacher and sit just at the back.

The preacher was amazing! The crowd was in a great mood.
But, tummies started rumbling and the people wanted food.

Now, can you believe it! 5000 people were there,
and not one of them had brought a bite of food to share!

The boy looked at his bread and fish. Oh dear, there wasn't a lot!
But, he took it to the preacher and gave him all he'd got.

The preacher took his offering, closed his eyes and said a prayer.
Miraculously there was food for everyone – with 12 baskets to spare!

So, bring the little that you have – it might not be very much, but, in the preacher's hands it will be transformed by his wondrous touch.

The little that you offer will be welcomed and will definitely increase!
Best of all – you'll be blessed and have everlasting peace!

27   100 points

I had the weirdest dream the other night as I lay snuggled up in bed.
I stood outside the pearly gates and realised that I was dead!
St Peter took one look at me and this is what he said.

"Hello Joy, I hadn't realised that you'd died...
Now, you are here you'll want to come inside.
But, what makes you think that I should let you in?
You need to score 100 points and be free from sin."

Well, in my dream I'd gone prepared.
So this 100 point thing hadn't got me scared.
For in my hands I'd got my C.V.
of all the things that made me, ME.

"So, Peter", I said "Now let me see.
I am a regular attender at the U.R.C".
"That's great", said Pete hanging on to heaven's door.
"That earns you half a point - to begin your score".

"Well I'm the secretary and have been for ages,
and I do it all for love - cos I never get no wages".
Peter smiled at me just like a saint,
and said "If you think you're coming in...
... well forget it cos you ain't".
"I'm sorry if this is mean and surely disappoints,
but being Church secretary only scores two points".

"How about arranging flowers and typing up the rota?"
"Forget it!" said Pete "that doesn't change things one iota".
"Well what about praying? And me with dodgy knee joints".
St Peter smiled fondly and said "O.k. that's three points".

"Do I get credit for all the hymns that I've sung,
and all the prayers that I've prayed?
And surely I must earn some points,
for all the cups of tea I've made?
And what about all the people,
I've known and cared for and befriended?
The plants and animals that I've loved,
and so carefully tended?"

I was getting pretty panicky and feeling quite depressed.
"Peter, help me!" I implored "How can I become blessed?
Perhaps you can give advice or give me the nod.
For, the only way that I'll get in is by the Grace of God".

"That's worth 100 points!" St Pete said as he flung wide the
door.
"Welcome to Heaven! Come on in - don't worry any more".
And as I entered heaven, I heard all the angels cheer
"For it is by the Grace of God that you are saved to enter
here!"

A life in all its fullness,
was what Jesus promised to me.
But, instead a life that is too full,
is what it's turned out to be!

I'm just a girl who can't say no.
So, people will always ask...
Will I do this? Will I do that?
Will I take on this onerous task?

And, so my Christian life has been,
full and overflowing at the brim.
Which doesn't leave me time,
to read my Bible or pray or worship Him.

I think that people underestimate,
all the time spent – all the hours!
Selecting, choosing, buying
and arranging the Church's flowers.

The rotas that I've organised.
The meetings attended – all the chatter!
The coffee mornings – cups of tea made.
I suppose it must all matter?

I'm at the age where I feel I've done my time.
I've put all the hours in!
Flippin' 'eck– this full-life must be good.
Because there's precious little time for me to sin!

No time to ponder, no time to think.
No time to stand and stare!
No time to do the things I want.
No time for God or Prayer.

So, as I reach the end of a working life.
The time to finish my career.
I must learn to say 'no',
 to all those extra unwanted Church jobs,
and have a break for at least a year!

29   Give - act - pray

If we can give why don't we?
If we can act let's do!
If we can pray, it must be.
Give - act- pray - it's true.

Unconditional love,
is given by God to you.
Replicate this love,
in all you say and do.

Love can only take us so far,
then hard work must kick in.
Give -act- pray.
Good advice that's where we can begin.

IF is a great big question.
IF is an amazing ask.
Are we worthy of the challenge?
Can we accept this IF task?

If we are friends of Jesus?
If in Gods' image made?
If we are loving Christian?
Can we share Christian Aid?

If we in our uniqueness?
If we can share our voice?
If we can influence others ?
Then as Christians that must be our choice!

IF we can GIVE.
IF we can ACT.
IF we can PRAY.
GIVE - ACT - PRAY- that's all I'll say.

A little gift from me to you - use it as you will - maybe tweak it
to suit you?
Put in your Church magazine? email to others?
Spread the word about the IF campaign.
Enough Food For Everyone - enoughfoodif.org
www.enoughfoodif.org/

I knew that you were feeling sad,
and knowing that me sad too.
So, today I'm sending positive thoughts,
and saying a prayer, or two, for you.

Carpe diem - seize the day.
Make this day your own!
Remember our God is with you.
You need never feel alone.

Stick a smile on your face.
Say "Hello" or sing out loud.
For there is silver lining,
hiding behind every grey storm cloud.

Remember, you have a loving family,
and friends who care and love you too!
Squash those worries, fears and doubts.
Remember, God loves you.

This day is just another day.
A gift like all of the rest.
Smile, have hope, embrace this day.
It might be one of your best!

Praying helps when feeling low.
Chocolate is a great boost too!
Whatever it takes to lighten your load...
...and remember, I said a prayer for you.

God bless you as you face your day.
May your spirits rise and lift.
Seize this day - enjoy it.
God gave you TODAY as a gift!

31   <u>I'm saying a prayer for you today.</u>

I'm saying a prayer for you today.
I'm lighting a candle too.
I pray that God will be at your side,
in all that you are going through.

I don't know what you are suffering.
I know I cannot be there.
But, I can pray for comfort for you,
and commit you to God's care.

I pray that there will be calmness,
and reassurance of mind.
I pray that you will find comfort,
and fresh hope you will find.

I pray for a positive outcome,
whatever that may be.
I'm saying a prayer for you today.
That from your worries you'll be free.

I'm lighting a candle for healing.
I'm praying that you will cope.
I'm sending you God's blessing.
I'm praying a prayer of hope.

32   Jesus is a linedancer too

Each night as I kneel by my bedside.
I hang my head in prayer.
I pray to my Lord to help me.
But He, He never seems to hear.
I pray that He will help me.
To be graceful supple and slim.
For, I wanna be a linedancer,
and dance in the footsteps of Him.

Chorus   For Jesus is a line dancer too.
                I know this to be true.
                He is the way, the true grapevine.
                Follow behind Him, now get in line.
                For Jesus is a linedancer too.
                Jesus is a line dancer too.

He gave me a perfect body.
It got messed up along the way.
The cussin 'and drinkin and lovin',
S'made me the woman I am today.
I ain't got no sense of direction.
I cain't tell my left from my right.
But I'll just keep on tryin',
Line dancin' evr'y Tuesday night.

For twelve months I've had lessons.
For twelve months and a day.
I still cain't do all them footsteps.
But, I love it so that's O.K.
I cain't do the cowboy motion,
the boogie or bus stop at all.
But, I can kick and stomp and yell,
and I can shout "Yee ha! Y'all!"

When I dance the Honky Tonk cowboy,
I think of the people he knew.
The publicans and the sinners.
People like me and you.
I think of those Honky Tonk people,
who followed my Saviour in line.
For they know He was the way and the life.
He is the true grapevine.

Despite the pain in my back.
Never mind my achy breaky knee.
I'll follow my leader in dancin',
 and dance for eternity.
When my line dancing days are over,
and I've got my eternal rest.
You'll find me line dancing' in Heaven.
and I shall be dancin' the best.

When my time on earth is over,
when I've had my three score years and ten,
I'll be linedancin' in Heaven with Jesus.
For ever and ever... Amen.

33   Lord, let me be…

Lord, let me be a gentle breeze, a zephyr of your care.
Let me drift your loving word around, throughout the
atmosphere.
Use me as a hurricane, or a strong and powerful cyclone.
So, that I can spread your love around, wherever I am blown.

Lord, let me be a flickering flame, to light a person's way.
Let me be a beacon of service, blazing each and every day.
Use me as a raging fire, a conflagration in humanity's souls.
So that I can kindle your love in us and we shall become
whole.

Lord, let me be a drop of dew, to moisten an arid land.
Let me irrigate people's barren lives, so your peace they'll
understand.
Use me as a torrential flood, an ocean of your grace.
So that I can cascade your love to all, in each and every place.

Lord, let me be a twinkling star, a sign for all to view.
Let me rotate your power around the earth, let me shine for
you.
Use me as a brand new world, a great and glorious earth.
So that I can create your love anew in each and every birth.

Lord, let me be a loaf of bread, a goblet of fine red wine.
Let me be a symbol of sacrifice, of your life laid down for
mine.
Use me as an offering, a covenant from you to the world.
So that I can be a sign to all of your amazing love unfurled.

34   May the clouds of yesterday

May the clouds of yesterday disappear in the sunshine of
today.
May your days be full of sunbeams instead of hazy grey.
May God keep you and bless you and take away your fears.
May God comfort and embrace you and wipe away your tears.
May your heart be filled with courage instead of bleak despair.
Remember, God is there at the end of each and every prayer!

35   Poems written for a Prayer Walk

"Sit with me", the Lord said.
"Talk with me awhile.
You've not conversed with me for ages,
tell me your concerns, my precious child".

"Talk to me of your burdens.
Be frank and open up your heart.
You need to be honest with me,
for our dialogue to start".

"Find time to pray, my child,
I'm here for you each day.
I long to help and encourage you,
but you need to take the time to pray".

"Share your sad times with me.
Celebrate the good!
My love and care is there for you,
as I promised that it should".

"Bring your burdens to me,
I'll banish them away,
I'll lift your spirits, calm your soul.
I'll listen when you pray".

I was supposed to go on a prayer walk,
but, I sat in the sun instead.
I read my Bible, prayed my prayers
whilst the sun anointed my head.
I basked in God's glory and goodness.
I felt the warmth of God's blessings and love.
The sun was a symbol of God's bounty.
His promises warming me from above.

36   Regularly as moon tides

Regularly as moon tides, every month it comes again.
This bloody monthly visitor is a real period...pain!

It started way back, long ago, I really do believe,
that this curse upon us women started with our sister, Eve.

And throughout all the ages,
women suffer with low back ache,
headaches, tummy pains and nausea,
 all for womanhood's sake.

You get that nagging feeling, you really don't feel well.
The horrid bloody messes and that horrid bloody smell.

So imagine how you'd feel, the heartache and the tears.
If, like that woman in the Bible, you had bled for 12 long years.

Back in Bible times there was not a lot of pain relief,
and bleeding women were unclean.
 Can you imagine her grief?
Not welcome at the temple. So, where could she go to pray?
Seeking out physicians that cannot help.
                              What a heavy price to pay!
But...wait there is a healer.
He's coming to our town.
If only she could touch him.
Feel the power flowing from his gown.

The miracle happened straightway. A healing gave her peace.
That unstoppable haemorrhage...Well it simply had to cease.

The healer turned and looked around,
He'd felt the power go.
That miraculous charge had left him,
 and had cured that woman's flow.

He was on his way to heal another.
 Jairus' daughter who was sick.
On the way - he'd chanced upon this woman,
 who had acted, quick.

'Where has my power gone?'
Jesus asked the crowded throng.
The woman cowered in the dust.
She thought she had done wrong.

'Rabbi, I knew if I touched your garment,
that healing would come from you.
I knew that you are merciful,
and the father's love is in all that you do'.

'Woman, your faith has cured you.
Go home for you are made well'.
What joy was in her heart that day!
How can we hope to tell?

So, a lesson here in this story.
Remember, Jesus still heals today.
Whatever ails befall you,
ask for healing when you pray.

We still have our women's ailments.
They often take their toll.
So, give your period pains to Jesus,
and thank God for Paracetamol.

Bring your problems to Jesus,
flagging spirits He revives.
Ask and it will happen ,
for Jesus is Transforming Lives!

37   The Lord's my pilot

(can be sung to The Lord's my Shepherd – Crimond)

The Lord's my pilot, I'll not fear.
He makes me brave to fly.
In heavens of blue, he leadeth me,
and jets me through the sky.

My nerves he doth restore again,
and me to cope doth make.
Within the skies of turbulence,
even for his own name's sake

Yea though I fly through turbulence,
yet will I fear no ill,
for thou art with me, radar too,
and computer guidance will comfort still.

An airline meal thou hast furnished me.
And after I'll have a doze.
My tongue thou dost with rescue remedy anoint,
and my tea cup overflows

Goodness and mercy all my flight,
shall surely follow me.
And on God's plane I will not fear
but enjoy free films and free TV.

38   Wages of sin

I opened up my pay advice slip,
and what I saw there took away my breath,
for in the net pay section,
I read... 'the wages of sin are death'.

I wondered - what sins I had committed,
to have to pay such a heavy price?
Murder? Idolatry? Deception?
Or maybe not being so very nice?

I know that my main vice is chocolate,
and greed is a sin at any rate.
But, is death to be the punishment,
for eating chocolates before it's after eight?

I might have told an odd white lie.
Well... maybe one or two.
Perhaps, my fibs weren't all pure white,
but the colours of the rainbow hue?

I'll admit to passing on gossip,
when I've got a juicy tale to tell.
But surely the re-telling of a rumour,
shouldn't condemn me to hell?

I know that I can be sharp-tongued,
and I can have a nasty streak.
And when virtues were handed out in Heaven...
...well they forgot to give me 'meek'.

But how can I redeem myself?
This pay-slip really disappoints.
How can I get back in God's good books,
and earn some loyalty points?

I feel like these sins are just too much,
and I'd like for them to shift.
Wait …hang on a second…
I've just read here about God's great free gift!

In the credits column of my pay-slip,
someone's written - see Romans 6 verse 23.
And I know that I can claim God's forgiveness,
because Jesus died for me!!!

So, although I worked hard on these sins,
they can be written off - wipe the slate!
For God's free gift of eternal life,
is a fantastic bonus tax rebate!!

Romans 6 23 - For the wages of sin is death, but the gift of
God is eternal life in Christ Jesus our Lord.   NIV

For sin pays its wage - death; but God's free gift is eternal life
in union with Christ Jesus our Lord.   Good News Bible

39   We three trees

(Can be sung to the tune – We three kings)

We three trees in the greenwood do grow.
the power of creation we all know.
Father God above us.
We know that He loves us.
We worship Him here below.

Chorus -
O trees in the greenwood growing strong.
Singing God's praises all day long.
A sign of God's power,
every hour.
Join us in our worship song!

I'm Bruce the Spruce, of trees I'm the best.
My wish is to be a treasure chest.
It will be my pleasure,
to hold jewels and treasure.
Then I shall be truly blest

Chorus –
O trees in the greenwood growing strong,
Singing God's praises all day long.
A sign of creation,
to every nation.
Join us in our worship song!

I'm Freda the Cedar, I want to be,
a mighty ship sailing over the sea.
Over waves I will far go,
with kings and their cargo.
Then I'll be a happy tree.

Chorus –
O trees in the greenwood growing strong,
Singing God's praises all day long.
A sign of God's grace,
in every place.
Join us in our worship song!

I'm Ever Green; I don't want to leave,
To go from this place would make me grieve.
I'll be a sign for the world.
of God's love unfurled,
So everyone will believe.

Chorus –
O trees in the greenwood growing strong,
Singing God's praises all day long.
A sign of God's love,
from Heaven above.
Join us in our worship song!

We three trees in the greenwood do grow,
the power of creation we all know.
Father God above us.
We know that he loves us.
We worship him here below.

When life is turning pear shaped,
then let your response be prayer shaped.

When life is hurtling all downhill,
then turn to prayer, let your anxieties still.

When troubles come knocking at your door,
then turn to prayer or a good friend, more.

When everything seems all too much,
then seek calmness with prayer and such.

When illness is defeating you and you don't care,
then find others to pray and they will share.

When all seems lost and you have no hope,
then remember others will pray for you to cope.

When life is turning pear shaped,
then let your response be prayer shaped.

I'm trying to be a good Christian
But often my life seems such a mess.
I pray God, 'Can you help me?'
He answers 'You're a work in progress'.

I've committed all the deadly sins.
Seven of them, I must confess.
I pray 'God stop me sinning'
He answers 'You're a work in progress'.

I'm a greedy, hungry person.
I don't understand the concept of less.
I pray God 'Stop me scoffing'.
He answers 'You're a work in progress'.

I lust after handsome film stars.
George Clooney is the one, I like the best.
I pray 'God can you tame me? '
He answers 'You're a work in progress'.

I am an envious person.
Coveting other's clothes, shoes, dress...
I pray 'God curb my desires'.
He answers 'You're a work in progress'.

I am a prideful person
Boasting I am better than the rest.
I pray 'God stop my big-headedness'.
He answers 'You're a work in progress'.

I am a slothful person.
Can't be energised to perform, except under duress.
I pray 'God be Lucozade to me'.
He answers 'You're a work in progress'.

I am an angry person.
Moody, nasty, and full of grumpiness.
I pray 'God make me pleasant'
He answers 'You're a work in progress'.

According to my adult children,
my moaning only causes ME stress.
I pray 'God stop me wanting to throttle them!'
He answers 'You're a work in progress'.

I AM a work in progress.
God's got his work cut out with ME.
I'm a chicken – should be an eagle.
I should be soaring high and free.

'So, please God, keep working on me.
I ask that me you'll bless.
Let me live up to my name and be Joy – full!
Amen from your own work in progress'.

Women's problems

Women's problems – you have either them, are going to have them or know someone who has them. Just embrace them! The problems! Recently, a woman told me that she had heard me perform one of my mammie gram poems and she felt that she needed to go for the test. A small tumour was found and dealt with.

I was very touched that one of my 'daft poems' had been useful in this way...so I wrote another poem – smear campaign because smear tests are important too!

42   Coming out of the water closet

It's time for me to come out of the water closet.
I have a wee problem you see.
I need to be frank and forthright,
and admit that I always need the w.c.

I've been to the incontinence clinic.
At my age, what could be sadder?
Than to be told I have a very common problem,
and that I have an over active bladder.

I'm exercising my pelvic floor muscles.
I'm drinking decaffeinated tea.
But, I don't that it's really working,
as I'm always needing to rush off for a wee.

The sound of a babbling brook,
a leaking tap will set me off.
And I need to cross my legs,
if I have to sneeze or have to cough.

When out walking in Derbyshire,
if I've disappeared - where will I be?
I'm usually communing with nature;
you'll find me crouching behind a tree

So, meanwhile I'm doing my best.
I realise my problem may be here for a while.
All I can do is panic buy Tena Lady's.
Buy one get one free and I've got a stockpile.

43   I used to be a temple

My body used to be a temple,
a shrine to womankind,
where acolytes and disciples worshipped,
at the altar of my mind.

My face was an inspiration,
it launched a thousand ships.
Artists argued over the correct shade,
to paint my luscious lips.

But...like all temples of long ago.
I too have had my day.
And, like those long forgotten shrines,
I've started to decay.

My body now is old and ruined,
with bits that droop and sag.
I was a fine, bright, new silk purse,
but now I'm just an old bag.

My body now is not so pert, to gravity I must succumb.
Everything points southwards now...especially my bum!

If history was herstory,
would we change the words that label?
Would every month we womenstruate?
Would we be pre-womenstruable?

Would we never be tempera-womental?
Never be hersterical?
Would our lives be more henriched?
Would they be more purposeful?

Would we suffer from womenses?
Would we delight in our womanhood cause?
Would we look forward to the end of our womenstrual cycle?
And celebrate our womenopause?

I wonder why our female conditions,
are prefixed by masculine words.
Menstruation, Menopause. Hysterectomy
it really is hysterically absurd.

These male words make me angry.
My head begins to whirl.
Lift up the feminist flag.
Let's celebrate and enjoy being a girl!

45   Mammies

I've got to get my mammies grammed.
I'm really not too keen,
to have my mammies,
squashed inside a great big photo' machine!

I've got to get my mammies grammed.
I'm really not quite sure.
So, I'm practicing at home,
by trapping them inside the refrigerator door!

I've got to get my mammies grammed.
That big machine really is the pits.
To get a decent photograph,
it just has to squish and squash my tits!

I've got to get my mammies grammed.
The screening unit isn't too far.
Time to shower and pamper myself,
and get dressed-up in my bestest bra!

The technicians are highly qualified.
I've heard they've all been to "Uni".
But if I'm to get my bosoms out,
I'd prefer it to be for George Clooney!

46   Mammies again

I can't believe it's been three years,
where has all that time gone?
It's time again to get my mammies grammed.
I don't anticipate it'll be that much fun!

The waiting room is state of the art,
with coffee and the latest glossy magazines.
I think they are there to take your mind off...
...those great big whopping machines!

The last time, I went, 3 years ago.
The technician looked me straight in the eye.
I looked back, gulped and wondered,
if I should laugh or cry?

'I'm sorry', she said, 'Gulp' said I
'I'm sorry to be such a pain...
...but your picture came out blurry
and I really need to take the photo again.'

'That's OK – no problem', I replied
and with relief I started to laugh.
'You see I know it often happens.
that I don't take a very good photograph!'

So remember despite being squished and squashed
and your mammies in a big machine slammed!
Respond to that appointment – is my advice
and go and get your mammies grammed!

The letter came this morning.
Well, flipping 'eck. I'll be damned!
Surely, it's not that time again...
...To go and get my mammies grammed.

I know that it's important.
I know it must be done.
But squishing, squashing mammies,
just really ain't much fun.

I 'm sure it's only just two years,
since the last time my mammies were grammed.
I haven't have time to psyche myself up,
and prepare for them to be in a machine...jammed.

I know the staff will offer me coffee,
and the latest glossy magazines.
But that only delays the time until;
I meet the mammie gramming machines.

I wish someone would invent a way,
to gramme mammies without any pain.
But until they do, I'll grin and bear it.
Mammie gramming time is here again!

It really is important.
You know you really must.
Go for that appointment...
...and let the professionals check your bust.

I've been pondering and thinking lately,
and a thought has only just occurred,
that of all the poems I've written,
there isn't one about smear tests - not a word.

It's not that I've ignored smear tests.
Of smears I'm not being disdainful.
But, I've been having them for years,
and they're really not that painful

I suppose it can be embarrassing,
waiting for the nurse with her spatula stick.
So I'm lying back and thinking of England,
just like good old Queen Vic!

The procedure is all over very quickly...
...but dare I be so bold?
To say...that the experience would be more pleasant,
if the instruments weren't so cold...?

So, don't lie there getting your knickers in a twist.
Remember that a smear test should not be missed.
So really I think it is for the best,
when that reminder letter comes,
make an appointment for the test!

Life

Some of the curiosities of life.

"Be careful what you wish for" was written as a summer message to colleagues and has since been used, by me, many times as a birthday greeting.
Inspiration often comes from comments that people make – "with you by my side every day is an adventure" was a phrase seen on a friend's Facebook post.

"I won't miss..." was written as a farewell poem when I was leaving the School that I worked at. Teachers may identify with this poem! I expect that some of the terminology is now defunct!

Some sad stuff is me remembering my Mum,
Lilian Margaret Garside 1921- 1972.

49   Be careful what you wish for...

Be careful what you wish for...
...for it just might come true.
So, it is with care that I wish,
only the very best for you.

I wish you a summer of calm and rest,
filled with happiness and sun!
I wish you evenings of tranquility,
or if you're up for it – lots of fun!

I wish you a garden that's an oasis,
with the fragrant scent of flowers.
I wish you an engrossing book to read,
to while away the hours.

I wish you time to take a step back.
to give your inner batteries time to renew.
I wish you a happy disposition,
and a positive point of view.

I wish God's blessing on you and yours.
I send these wishes true.
So, full of care I wish all the best,
and a happy summer to you!

50   I've had my leg over thirty seven times today

I've had my leg over thirty seven times today;
it's such a terrible chore.
I'm really struggling and I truly think...
...That I can't take it anymore.

I'm ok when it's horizontal,
then I'm alright and doing fine.
But you should hear me puff and pant,
at the slightest bit of an incline.

My knees are starting to throb now,
there's a sharp pain in my hip.
My breathing is getting deeper,
and my lady bits are giving me jip.

It's all the stopping and starting,
the getting off and having to push,
and all that pressure at the back,
is causing a throbbing in my tush.

When the going is horizontal,
then this really is a treat.
But, the ups and downs,
and the stops and starts make me admit defeat.

Ooh...we're coming to a conclusion.
Oh what bliss! What joy! I cried.
As I finished cycling along a sandy prom,
for a celebratory birthday bike ride.

Oh! What did you think this poem was?
Did you think that I was in luck?
Are you anticipating the last line?
What a mucky mind you have... mi'duck.

I won't miss helping children putting on lots of winter
hats and gloves.
        But, I will miss your smiley faces!
I won't miss lining up and all the pushing and the shoves.
        But, I will miss playing at Mr Wolf and chases!

I won't miss practising the Christmas play,
that changes each and every day,
with extra things added to give everyone a chance.
I won't miss practising each and every dance.
        But, I will miss the sparkle of Christmas!

I won't miss the bogey that's been mined with precision.
It was one of the things that helped me make my
decision!
I won't miss the accidents – the soggy wet pants.
    But, I will miss the Butterflies and the Butterfly dance!
I won't miss the TA that comes rushing in at half past
eight.
    But, I will miss the times when she always stayed late.
I won't miss the teasing and the rude remarks.
    But, I will miss the fun and the jokes and the larks!

I won't miss CLLD, paired talk and ECAT.
    But, I will miss the times we had a spontaneous chat.
I won't miss the rhyming basket or the chatterbox.
I won't miss the colds, sniffles or the yearly bout of
chickenpox.
I won't miss the MATHS now called PRSN.
      But, I will miss the magic of a child counting to ten.
I won't miss the collating of info and data.
But, I will miss the child who says 'see you later, alligator!'

I won't miss the curriculum, the plans – all that typing!
I won't miss the bottoms that want wiping!
But, I will miss the pleasure of meeting all kinds.
I will miss the challenge of educating young minds.
I will miss the fun of learning new things too.
I will miss looking at all things anew.
I will miss discovering things with surprise,
and looking at the world, in wonder, through a child's eyes.

I won't miss tidying up the cupboard – it's a job that I hate.
And – anyway – a few days later- it's back in a terrible state!
I won't miss the tiredness and sitting on the floor.
I won't miss the cold from the often left-open door.
I won't miss the tantrums - I won't miss the tears.
But, I will miss the fun of working in Early Years.

I know that you'll all be too busy to miss me
with all the learning and work to be done.
But, perhaps when you have a spare minute,
you'll remember the laughs and the fun!

So, stop what you're doing when you are able,
pause for a little while,
remember the good times we had together,
and remember me with a smile!
I'll think of you with fond memories.
I'll remember the laughter and the fun.
But...now it's time for me to leave...
...my work at this School is done.

When I'm feeling down at heart,
and the day is dull and dreary.
What better way to cheer me up,
then to watch an episode of,
The Little House on the Prairie.

The characters are like a second family to me.
Their days are always filled with fun.
They do their chores, run in the meadow,
and their days are full of sun!

There's Ma and Pa, Laura and Carrie too,
 in that Little House on the Prairie,
baby Charles, who died, baby Grace who's new,
and the eldest daughter, Mary.

No matter what life throws at them,
they always seem to cope.
Their lives are full of sunshine,
of laughter, love and hope.

This is the box that contained...would you believe...
...the pill that wasn't used and so you were conceived.

This is the box that contained the pregnancy test.
That showed you were on the way and we were truly blessed.

This is the box that contained the nappies, paraphernalia and pram.
That cluttered the house...ad nauseam.

This is the box that contained the photos, greeting cards and hospital tags.
Your first lock of hair, first Clark's shoes preserved in brown paper bags.

This is the box that contained the Christmas toy and building blocks.
That you left unnoticed and preferred to play with the box.

This is the box that obtained the packed lunch that you took to school on your very first day.
That can home uneaten because you were too busy, at play.

This is the box that contained the red Raleigh bike that caused such a fuss.
When you got it to celebrate passing your eleven plus.

This is the box that obtained the players extra strength that made you feel grown up.
That you smoked, behind the bike shed, but only caused you to throw up.

This is the box that contained the exam papers that made you feel stressed.
The results of which proved that you were one of the best.

This is the box that contained the ring that was to change your lifestyle.
That caused you to cry, shout, curse, laugh and smile.

This is the box that contained the family and home in it.
On a street full of other boxes all mortgaged up to the limit.

This is the box that contained the wine that you drank sparingly.
But only on days that contained the letter D.

This is the box that contained the vitamins that you take knowing.
You need them, at this stage of life, just to keep going.

This is the box that contained the morning chat shows, news & views on which you depend.
Your instant background noise and your constant friend.

This is the box that contained the earthly remains... for you've ceased to be. A life measured in many boxes. God bless R.I.P.

Every day is an adventure,
with you by my side.
New things to discover,
life's a roller coaster ride.

Let's get out there together!
Search the whole world wide.
I can do anything,
with you by my side.

Exploring daily wonders,
with you by my side.
Partners, sharing as equals.
Perfect friend and guide.

Together we are awesome!
Your love fills me with pride.
Every day is an adventure,
because you are by my side.

55   When

When you're feeling stressed out and you can't stand the
strain.
When it's all too much and life is a pain.
When you're feeling hormonal or just at your worst.
When if you don't scream out loud you feel that you'll burst.

When some man has hassled you, moaned at you or annoyed.
When you feel that life is yawning out like a great big void.
When you're feeling hung over and the worse for wear.
When the world is against you and 'they' don't care.

When you don't feel like work and your job seems boring.
When you look like the cat's dinner - instead of looking
alluring.
When you can't go shopping 'cause you've got no money.
When it's raining outside instead of being sunny.

Then here's what you must do to make you feel great -
eat lots and lots and lots of chocolate!

Alternate endings - if you don't like chocolate!
Then here's what you must do to make you feel fine
get a big packet of crisps and open a bottle of wine!

Then here's what you must do to banish your cares
try singing your heart out or, better still, say your prayers!

Then here's what you must do to make you feel carefree
go into the kitchen and make a nice cup of tea!

When I awoke this morning,
my first thought was of you.
So, I pray that God is there for you,
in everything you do.

I'm sad because you are sad.
So, this is what I pray,
that God uplifts you, cheers you,
and you have a better day, today.

A day that's full of promise.
A day that's full of hope.
A day when you are powerful,
and with everything can cope.

A bright day that is golden
is what I pray for you.
God delivers...ask Him.
You know that this is true.

God bless you today and every day.
Even when the day is dark, walk in the light of Jesus.

Working full-time is hard work.
It really is a chore!
I'm getting too old for this lark.
I don't want it anymore.

My co-workers are all wonderful.
The atmosphere is really great.
Getting home each day exhausted,
is the bit that I really hate!

My housework gets left 'till Saturday.
The house just gets into a mess.
And...cleaning at the weekend.
Well, I really couldn't care less!

So, roll on back to part time hours.
I can't stand this hectic pace.
I need the time to wash and clean,
and put everything back in its proper place.

No time to cook some proper meals.
Just quickly eating beans on toast.
I get in too late to prepare the veg,
and cook us a tasty roast.

Hobbies are a thing of the past.
Leisure time - I'm out of luck.
I've barely time to write a poem,
or even check the latest on Facebook.

But, wait - there's light at the end of the tunnel.
This busy time is coming to an end.
I'll stick to part-time in future.
Full-time's driving me around the bend.

I won't be working full-time anymore.
I can manage on part-time pay.
It gives me time to recharge my batteries.
To work and rest and play!

58 A song for my Mum - Aura lee tune (aka Love me tender)

I can't believe the time has flown,
since that day you died.
Did you know how much you're missed?
Did you know how much I cried?

You left so quick, there was no chance,
for me to say goodbye.
I think of you with an aching heart,
and try hard not to cry.

Why is life so short a span?
No time for things to do.
If I could have this time again,
I'd tell you that I love you.

I miss you, more than I can say.
I hate that we're apart.
When you died, part of me died too.
There's an empty ache in my heart.

Life moves on. I've done with grief.
Put all of this aside.
But a day like today...I remember,
and think of that day you died.

One day, we will be together.
How happy I shall be.
Dancing with you in heaven.
Together my Mum and me!

And a sad poem too...

I can't believe that you've been gone so many years!
I remember you with fondness and a few tears.
Forty two years have gone by...
Since last we said good bye.
I think about you often...in my prayers.

If I knew that day, that it would be your last,
would I have clung to you and held you fast?
Would I have hugged and kissed you?
Told you how much I'd miss you?
I can't believe that forty two years have flown past.

You were so very happy, that last day.
Gone out with such great news to say.
A new grandson's birth.
You were the happiest grandma on earth.
Why did you have to go, why couldn't you stay?

The void you left has been filled by many others.
Children, grandchildren, friends, husband and lovers.
But, you were the one who loved me first.
You loved me at my best and at my worst.
No one can really fill the gap that's left by mothers.

So, Mum, on this your anniversary day.
When I meet you again ...what will I say?
So many years have passed.
My life has moved on so fast.
I hope you hug me, in your old usual way.

I hope that in heaven, you are looking at me.
I hope that you are proud of what you see.
I've heard it said by others,
that we turn into our mothers.
If that is true how happy I would be!

Oddities

I put these poems in this section simply because I couldn't think what other category they fitted in with.

59   A cautionary tale

Ronnie Rice (no relation) a naughty boy, who nearly burnt the house down - with his sister trapped inside.

This is the tale of Ronnie Rice.
A boy (it's said) who wasn't often nice.
On bonfire night, the little louse,
deliberately set fire to his parent's house.

He built the bonfire next to the shed.
and pretty soon the conflagration spread.
Along the fence the flames they shot,
 soon it got infernally hot!

Up the conservatory walls the flames quickly flickered,
whilst little Ronnie calmly snickered.
Tongues of flame, licked higher and higher,
Ron danced 'round and 'round the fire.

He thought this was the best of games,
as he rushed around and fanned the flames.
For trapped inside was his sister, Sue,
Not aware of the fire...she hadn't a clue.

She was doing her homework the little swot
Whilst Mum and Dad did the weekly shop.
She did her maths and drank her coffee,
hoping for a shopping surprise of bonfire toffee.

The thought of the toffee made her drool,
all over the sums she had done for School.
But...what was that smell all sooty and smoky,
that tickled her throat and made her feel choky?

Sue was a girl, who didn't waste time,
So, she promptly dialled nine, nine, nine.
Meanwhile, our Ron, the fire was stoking,
now the back door was burnt and the brickwork smoking.

Just then the Cavalry (well.... Mum and Dad),
arrived with the shopping and collared the lad.
He was walloped and frisked...and the little blighter,
was found in possession of his granddad's lighter!

Sirens shrieking, the fire engines did arrive,
smashing into their car (that they'd left on the drive).
The firemen were keen and from the wreckage jumped out,
and rapidly set about putting the raging fire out.

A handsome fireman, clad all in yellow,
saved our Sue – what a brilliant fellow!
He carried her out 'fireman style',
Sue gave him mouth to mouth for quite a while!

Her parent's smiled and sighed with relief,
then looked at the house – it was beyond belief!
Smoked had damaged the windows and doors
and most of the fire had gutted the floors.

Amongst it all stood a mournful Ron,
who couldn't believe what he had done.
It took many months to put things straight...
...the insurance company was irate.

For on the policy there was no cover,
for an act of arson by Sue's little brother.
Dad phoned them up and gave them a prod and
found that it was covered as "An act of Sod".

This proves that misprints, one should read...
...for you never know when a claim you might need!
Now, Ron is grounded in his bedroom,
he won't be allowed out until, at least, mid-June.

The only time he is permitted an outing,
is on Tuesday nights when he goes Scouting.
His parents think Scouts are really great,
but you just wait and wait and wait.
Little do they know...Ron is up to his tricks?
for he's learning to make sparks by rubbing two sticks!

Moral – The moral to this tale –   is you really shouldn't trust,
                    naughty boys with materials that combust.
Or   -   Ponder this tale, O reader gentle,
                    If you trust boys, like Ronnie, you must be mental.

60   Bulwell and Sutton on Sea.

There's a community known as Bulwell Village,
that's noted for friendship and fun.
It's a great place to visit or live in,
and well-loved by each and every one!

Bulwell Village is most friendly and sociable.
It's really a great place to be.
The only thing that could improve it,
 is if it could be moved nearer to the sea.

We have got ponds in one or two gardens,
and the River Leen is as clean as can be.
We've a water feature called Bulwell Bogs.
But really it's not quite like the sea.

So, some of us Bulwell Village people,
without any fuss, bother or impropriety,
decided we'd form a friendly association -
The Sutton on Sea Appreciation Society.

Our Bulwell Village hand of friendship,
is extended during this time of Diamond Jubilee.
What a great place for all of us to celebrate,
with our friends at Sutton-on-Sea!

So, raise your glasses let us make a toast.
God Bless our Queen on her Jubilee!
Bless Bulwell Village and all of her folk!
And God Bless Sutton on Sea!

It always seems to happen,
as I watch a repeat of 'Frost' or 'Morse',
that half way into it - I start to nod,
and then I'm fast asleep of course!

I'll be following the plot very carefully,
accompanied by a glass or two of wine,
and you can bet my eyes will be closing
when the little hand reaches half past nine!

I like to watch Midsomer Murders.
I quite like Lewis too.
But, I don't get to see the ending,
of the murderer - I haven't got a clue!

Now, Poirot, he's a great detective,
with his lovely Belgian patter.
But, I never find out 'whodunit'
as there's something up with my little grey matter!

I notice that they're repeating the Sweeney,
on ITV2 or is it BBC3?
Starting at 10 o'clock!! Well forget it.
That's far too late for me!

I'd love to watch a whole programme,
from the beginning until the conclusion.
To know what happened would be just brilliant,
and end my frustrated confusion!

If I was much better organised,
with a mind in better order.
I'd remember to find a blank tape,
and bung it into the video recorder.

But...wait... Midsomer Murders in the afternoon!
I've seen it written in the Radio Times.
Now, If I remember to sit and watch on my next day off,
I can find out at last who committed the crimes!

62   Giant Cacti

It was the Saturday after Christmas,
as I was driving through a Derbyshire Dale,
when suddenly...
...I saw a garden centre,
advertising a GIANT cactus sale!!!

Well...a giant cactus is something,
that I'd really like to see,
and I wondered if it would be all trimmed up,
just like a giant Christmas tree?

I looked around the garden centre,
all the shelves in there were stacked up high.
There were Poinsettias and Hyacinths,
and rows and rows of tiny baby cacti.

Nowhere was there a Saguaro,
or a massive cacti bush.
Had the giant cacti been snapped up,
in the post-Christmas rush?

So I asked a busy assistant,
and I didn't want to appear truculent.
"But, please luv can you tell me
where is the giant succulent?"

The assistant gave me a funny look,
and explained that the word 'giant' in the sign,
meant that they had lots and lots of pots,
of baby cacti beneath the Christmas pine.

She explained that this cactus sale,
could have been advertised as 'mega',
and thought perhaps it should have been,
to stop queries from silly beggars.

Now a baby cactus isn't much to look at,
it was 'lost' in its pot of pine.
So, I said 'No thanks' and made a swift exit.
A mini-cactus is something I'd have to decline.

So, if you see an intriguing sign
ignore it – as I know for a fact, I
can guarantee that in Derbyshire...
...there ain't any giant cacti!

63   I wouldn't be seen dead in that!

Waiting at North Berwick,
about to get on a Sea fari boat,
I had put on some massive waterproof trousers,
that came right up to my throat.

The woman in charge of kitting us out,
told me she hadn't a coat in my size.
I looked at all of the ginormous coats,
and couldn't believe my eyes.

Does she that that I'm big and fat?
Does she think my bum would look big in that?

She offered me a coat and that was much too big,
"You'll drown in that" she said.
"What I'll drown in it?
This is the coat that I will wear to drown? To be dead?"

Well it was extremely heavy,
and its pockets had been weighted down.
But really...was this what I'd want to wear...
... if I was destined to drown?

Could I not drown in designer swimwear?
Could I not have a fashionable hat?
For If I'm going to be drowned...
...Well, I wouldn't be seen dead in that!

No designer gear was on offer,
and realising what she'd said,
she meant that it was too big for me,
not that I'd be dead.

So when t' boat came in,
 and passengers swopped around,
A smaller life jacket that fitted me,
 was the first thing that was found.
A perfect fit – and guess what…?
… I wasn't drowned!

64   I've not read Fifty Shades of Grey.

I have a confession to make,
there's something I have to say.
I think I'm the only woman in England,
who's not read Fifty Shades of Grey.

I downloaded a sample onto my kindle,
but gave up after page twenty three.
To quote Boy George (on sex),
well... I'd rather have a cup of tea.

I flicked through a paper copy,
thought I try to read it again.
But... I really got turned off,
when I got to the red room of pain.

Maybe I'm too old for this book.
I'm past it, as this book doesn't appeal.
I can't get my knickers in a twist,
for the fictional Mr Steele.

I'll stick with Nordic noir;
Stig Larson's the one for me.
Or maybe Stephen King...
...or the nation's book of poetry.

65   Passport photos

A fiver for a photo!
That's really too much money.
For a picture that makes you look odd,
or even downright funny!

You're not allowed to smile.
You have to stare off into space.
You have to have your ears on display,
and try to keep a perfectly straight face!

You cannot have a fringe,
or any kind of fancy hair-do.
This photo shows you at your worst.
It does even look like you!

The chair always needs adjusting.
You need to move the curtains back.
The fluorescent light drains you of colour.
Not smiling makes your face look slack!

The flash can be quite blinding,
leaving you seeing floating dots before your eyes.
And you never know when the flash is coming,
so you end up with a mad look of surprise!

To get your pose just right, is harder that you thought.
Is it worth all of this hassle, just to renew your old passport?

And then there's the form to fill-in.
A letter in every box and space.
Someone has to sign to say that they know you
and this awful photo really is your face!

66   Piranha!

Some people look at me and think I'm vicious,
while others suppose that I look cruel.
But, I look hard enough, I do,
when I'm out with my School.

Some people hear the world 'piranha',
and it gets them all in a panic,
'cause they assume that me and my mates
are some kind of hooligan fish that's gone manic!

Some people say if fishes were people,
then I'd be just like Vinnie Jones.
They imagine that I'll take one look at 'em,
and strip their flesh right down to their bones,

Now, some people believe that I'm evil,
while others think my species is barbarian.
But, I just really want you all to know,
that some piranha are strictly vegetarian.

Please, let me set the record straight,
about my being a truly kind veggie piranha.
I don't crave human flesh at all.
I'd much rather have a nice banana!

Or, what about some nice endive salad?
Just the job to keep piranhas trim and slim.
Throw me some tasty Lollo Rosso,
and I'll tear it limb from limb.

67 <u>Playing the uke</u>
(can be sung to the tune Aura Lee – aka Love me tender)

I like to play the ukulele.
I like to play the uke.
If I get two chords right in succession.
Well I guess that would be a fluke.

Chorus   Ukulele, ukulele. of instruments you're the best.
       So why is it when I practice, my family shout give it a rest?

I'm learning to play the ukulele.
With a uke you will never be bored.
I've been trying hard since September.
But, have only got to grips with one chord.

If you should hear a melodious sound.
That surely that must be me.
Heavenly music on the air.
It's only me playing chord C.

George Formby is my hero.
He's such a cheeky chappy.
If I could play the uke like him.
Then I'd be very happy.

Ukulele ukulele
With a sound sweet as a lover's kiss.
I'd love to play like all the group...
...if only I'd practice.

I've never played a uke till now
I don't have a musical bent.
Never been interested...never tried
Never attempted a musical instrument.

My husband made a suggestion,
ooh! You are awful - not that kind.
He wants to team up with me.
He wants to pick my mind.
Now, I've been writing poems for ages,
I've hit the poetry golden seam.
I'm not sure how this will be,
if I became part of a poetry team.

Does he think that we are Lennon and McCartney?
I nearly said Simon and Garfunkel,
But, didn't as to make those rhyme,
I'd have to use a word like...carbuncle.
See – my rhyming muse has shifted.
I'm struggling to find rhymes that work.
I'm willing to try harder to be in this poetry partnership.
Rhyming work I will not shirk.

I get my inspiration from odd comments.
The muse hits me with thoughts that are daft.
I take snippets of overheard conversations,
and work my poetry witchcraft.
So, maybe two heads are better than one.
I suppose we could have double the fun.
O.K. we could be collaborators.
But, when all is said and done...

I'll say this at the beginning, listen up – I want to be heard.
I'll be your poetry partner, but, I want to write the last word.

Git along, you lonesome doggie.
Rocky, high, on the mountain side.
Git along, you poor ol' doggie.
Gonna get you back by my side.

Now, listen well my pardners, to this tale of grief and woe.
About a dog called Rocky, happened not too long ago.

Now, Rocky and his master, Ray,
went up the mountains of Superstition.
They walked all day, morn and afternoon,
it's a Thanksgiving tradition.

The trail was sure exciting,
with lots of interesting stuff.
Cacti, shrubs and snakes and things.
The trouble was the trail was rough.

Poor ol' Rocky got his feet sore. The pads were really cut.
He whimpered and he hollered, he was a poor ol' mutt.

Now, Rocky's a retriever.
A fine and sturdy hound.
A beast to be real proud of,
but he weighs a hundred and forty pound.

No way could he be carried, or forced to leave that place.
Ray tried every coercion, even smacked his little face.

Rocky stood and stood and stood there,
you could say he stood his ground.
He had no plans on leaving,
he was a stubborn hound.

The situation – it seemed hopeless.
Rocky wouldn't move – no siree.
At nightfall, Ray had to leave him.
So, he tied him to a tree.

The night was cold and miserable.
The coyotes they all howled.
But brave ol' Rocky stood his ground,
and to the coyotes, growled.

For two days, Rocky stayed there. It made ol' Raymond mad.
He took him food and water, and Band-Aids for his pads.

A whole bunch of friends tried helping,
with suggestions of what to do.
But poor ol' Rocky, he wouldn't budge,
seems his feet were stuck like glue.

A posse to help was organised.
Strong men – brave and true.
But, that ol' Rocky wasn't leaving,
there was nothing they could do.

Shooting him was an option. Ol' Ray...he had a gun.
But, to kill a pal like Rocky? Well. It just couldn't be done.

So, poor ol' Rocky stayed there,
with his poor ol' ruined feet.
The posse had to leave him,
they had to admit defeat.

But…listen up my pardners. Don't you fear nor fret.
Hope was still around there, we'll save ol' Rocky yet.

His help came from the heavens.
An helicopter from the state.
They winched Rocky up from off the trail,
and reunited him with his mate.

Now, Ray and Rocky are together,
they're as happy as can be.
Just remember this his story,
tell it to your family.

When walking in the mountains,
you better stick to the trail like me,
or like poor Rocky the doggie,
you'll spend the night tied to a tree.

Git along you lonesome doggie.
Rocky, high, stuck on the mountainside.
If you stand your ground on poorly feet,
gonna get you a chopper ride!

I'm going to tell you a story – I hope it's not too weird.
I'm trying not to freak you out – or even make you feel scared.
This story (poem) is about my friend, a truer, braver pal,
than you could ever hope to meet – my mate, Fearless Sal.

Sally went into the hedgerow,
 to investigate a commotion there.
When... out it leapt – the monster!
The grizzly grumpy sanglier.

'Oh my hens!' she shouted.
 'Oh my hens!' she yelped.
But no-one was around to assistez her,
not a soul who could have helped.

'Oh my hens!' she shrieked.
 'Oh my hens!' she cried.
So, that best thing to do was leg it to the hen-house.
The perfect place to hide!

The chickens never murmured,
 not a word was clucked or spoke.
The sanglier attacked the hen house door.
Thank Goodness it was made of sturdy oak!

What is a girl to do?
Hidden from the sanglier's sight.
She might have to find a safe perch,
and roost with the chickens tonight.

Eventually the boar soon got bored,
and off round Le Patis it toured.
So creeping out – quiet as a mouse,
our brave Sal could escape the hen house.

Afterwards – she said it was exhilarating!
She hasn't been chased for years!
What a pity that the pursuer,
was only a great big grizzly sanglier!

Still... it's a great story for Facebook.
An adventure to share with on-line friends.
And a new expletive was created.
OMH   - means 'Oh my hens!'

If it was me – I'd have said

'Oh my dickens.

          Look out chickens!'

Many years ago, when I first started work,
seems like it was the dark ages!
And the adding up and such was manually done,
 for nine pounds a week wages.

A colleague in the office came in with a gadget,
 that really mesmerised.
A pocket calculator that added,
subtracted, divided and multiplied!

These calculators were the latest thing,
 that were going the rounds.
And he had gone and bought one...
... for the sum of twenty-five pounds!

Now twenty five pounds was a fortune,
3 weeks wages at most.
But to have the latest calculator in 1971,
 that was a FAB boast.

A machine that did your calculations,
 was a great help with your sums.
And was marvellous for when you ran out,
 of using your fingers and your thumbs!

Now...technology has exploded,
and expanded and really gone berserk.
Think of how many gadgets that you have,
 at home, at school and work.

Computers, laptops, tablets, iPad.
Bet there's at least two or three you've got.
Flat screen, plasma, smart TVs and smartphones.
Bet you have got the lot!

And Twittering and Facebook,
and emailing all your friends.
Your time spent with technological gadgets,
really never ends!

Still...I ponder and think,
of all hundreds and thousands of screens,
That over the years,
my poor eyes must have seen.

And remember the warnings from my parents,
with a chuckle and some surprise.
After fifty–odd years of viewing ...
I still haven't got square eyes.

So, what is the point of this poem?
Bet, you're thinking OMG she's gone on for a while.
Well... thinking about all these ways of communicating...
...Surely the best way is still with a smile?

The day I got 3 holes in one,
I just couldn't believe my luck.
Because, I don't know the difference,
between a putter or a puck!

It usually takes me 5 or 6 shots.
I haven't much of a clue.
So, it was a surprise when I managed,
 to complete the first two holes in 2!

I turned to heaven for the next shot.
'God, don't leave me in the lurch,
everyone gets a hole in one here.
Can I have one – for all the years I've been to Church?'

I breathed deep, made my prayer,
studied the hole – and what a surprise!
The ball went in a one-shot wonder!
I could hardly believe my eyes!

The next hole, I called upon,
 the famous Ben Kenobi Jedi force.
The power was with me – a second hole in one!
And only part way around the course!

The crowd was tense.
I could feel them willing me on.
Would my luck hold,
or would the power be gone?

I breathed deep...again...and again.
'Keep calm and play golf' I cried.
Guess what? A third hole in one!
Never was there such Bulwell Village pride!

Who knows where the magic came from?
A lucky streak? Or God's or Jedi power?
But in Bulwell Village golfing history.
It was my finest hour!

Or rather my finest 5 minutes,
and I really wished that it would last.
My lucky streak, my magic power...
It had gone ...it had faded fast.

No matter how hard I tried,
I couldn't achieve any more outstanding goals.
The last 2 holes were my usual standard,
Taking 4 or 5 shots to reach the holes!

As, I grow older and time goes on.
I'll pass this legendary story on.
At Bulwell Village Golf in 2012.
when I got 3 consecutive holes in one!

So never mind the Olympics or the Jubilee
2012 – holes in one – Joy Rice – three!

73   The night that I met Elvis

The night that I met Elvis,
it really was a surprise!
There he was - the king himself.
I couldn't believe my eyes!

I was all shook up and said,
" Elvis, I thought that you were dead!"
"Huh huh" he answered gyrating his hips.
"Honey don't believe all the trash, you've read".

I may be a Lookilikey.
But, remember it's now or never.
Elvis may have left the building...
...but the king rocks on forever.

74   The Vill

Now, I'm from Bulwell Village, check it out you know it's true.
that I'm here as a representative of the Bulwell crew.

You know full well - that I'm from Bulwell.

The Vill's got all the amenities down to the last detail,
there's the library, shops, florists ... and a Co-op on the Vale.

Now it ain't perfect - but give the Vill nuff respect.

The Vill's got churches aplenty with groups that really thrill,
there's the URC, Baptists, Our Lady's and St. Mary's on the hill.

So come on let's chill - get on down to the Vill.

Don't forget there's Bulwell Common where the home-boys walk their dogs,
and if you want to have a paddle, then come on down to Bulwell Bogs.

It sure is a big thrill - to visit the Vill.

The Vill's a retail therapy heaven; we've got lots of shops,
Tesco's, Wilko's, Morrison's... and several charity shops.

You better be wise - and the Vill recognise.

And on Piccadilly, when the cherry trees are all a-flower.
Just be glad that you're in the Vill and celebrate Bulwell power.

You can't be passive - to belong to the Bulwell massive.

Now I may look odd and I might look silly.
Give me your respect bro', cos I'm the Poet of Piccadilly.

It sure is a privilege - to reside in the village.

So, if you want a poem, you don't have to look too hard,
for I'm called the Piccadilly Poet aka the Bulwell Bard.

I ain't no whipper-snapper - I'm the Bulwell rapper.
You know full well - that I'm from Bulwell.

My first and last attempt at rapping!

Songs have been written about walking.
Back to happiness or walking on the wild side.
You couldn't find a wilder, happier group,
then our healthy walking group, if you tried.

We meet every Monday morning,
on the high street at the bus stop,
and we set off on our walking adventures,
walking until we're fit to drop.

As we are striding out – we can chat,
on any subject or any old matter.
You can't beat a walk with good friends,
and you can't beat a good old natter.

These healthy walks are great,
and make us feel fitter and much fresher,
and one of the benefits of walking
is that it helps to reduce your blood pressure.

Feeling lethargic and need more energy?
Feel depressed and couldn't care less?
Well, walking will give you the feel good factor,
and it also helps to reduce your stress.

Healthy walking is good for you;
it's really a great pastime to start.
It's good to feel active, get some fresh air
and it's also great for your heart.

For a healthy heart - take exercise,
find something that suits you.
A daily walk, in the fresh air,
is really not too hard to do.

Healthy walking is good for you.
The benefits are many, so it's said.
A strenuous walk up hill and down dale,
and you'll certainly sleep better in your bed.

The British Heart Foundation,
 is really trying hard to please.
To supply the public with the facts
 to help fight heart disease.

Why not check out their website?
 www.bhf.org.uk - the info is there to see.
Great advice and tips to share,
so that you can live healthily.

Men

I have always liked Men. I'm surprised that I have only written a few poems about them. Recently, I realised that I hadn't written anything about my lovely Dad, Thomas Garside, who died at the young age of 56 when I was just 13 years old. So...after a couple of glasses of red wine drank on a recent Father's Day and...Hey presto! 2 Dad poems!

76 Alan Titchmarsh - can be sung to the tune Cwm Rhondda

Alan Titchmarsh is our hero,
we think he's our Mr. Right.
He can come to visit our gardens,
to sort out our potato blight.

Chorus   Alan Titchmarsh, Alan Titchmarsh
       We think that you're really great...really great.
       We think that you're really great.

Alan Titchmarsh is the expert,
who would like to really teach yer,
the correct positioning, that there is,
for his favourite water feature.

Alan Titchmarsh is a wonder,
the things that he knows about plants and weeds.
He can come to visit our gardens,
and share with us some of his seeds.

Alan Titchmarsh is a gardening genius,
with knowledge so far superior.
We'd like him to come and advise us,
what to do with our little grey area.

Alan Titchmarsh is really brilliant,
he's the best on Gardener's world.
Just the thought of his green fingers,
has made all of our toes curled.

Alan Titchmarsh is a man,
who is 'into' cultivation.
We'd like him to show us how,
he performs his propagation.

Alan Titchmarsh is most fantastic,
we think that he is sublime.
We can't wait to get our hands on him,
at the next Gardener's question time.

Alan Titchmarsh is the man,
with whom, we'd like to delve and dibble,
afterwards we'd take him home,
for a cup of tea...and maybe, even, a nibble?

Alan Titchmarsh is the salt of the earth,
he's just perfect in every way.
We'd like to be his gardening groupies,
and take him home with us today.

Alan Titchmarsh is the man,
who makes us hot, our blood starts to boil,
when he tells us with a knowing look,
that the secret is in the soil.

Alan Titchmarsh is the one we lust for,
our adoration we hope that he'll pardon.
For we'd just like to say to him,
"whatever the weather, enjoy your garden!"

I really don't think that I could be bored,
if left all alone with Harrison Ford.
I'd really like to tarry some,
with a naked, baby-oiled Harrison!

The only time that I'd let Harrison,
keep his hat and keep his kit on,
was if he dressed up as Indiana,
then I'd behave in an unseemly manner.

So, come on Harrison, for goodness sakes!
Stop messing with spiders and playing with snakes.
Come with me and make your mark,
and you can be the raider of my Lost Ark.

I've knelt, each night at my bedside and prayed,
that I could be the object of your Last Crusade.
But, the chances of your responding... fills me with gloom,
and turns my heart into the Temple of Doom.

Harrison, I'll just have to worship you from afar,
for I'm just a tiny satellite to your mega-star.
so I'll dream my dreams of being your mate,
whilst watching your videos and eating chocolate!

I've been sad since Bake-off finished.
So I was really pleased to know,
that the great BBC have given,
Paul Hollywood his own bread baking show.

I knead to see Paul hard at work.
Creating with yeast and flour,
traditional loaves, bloomers, malt loaf.
All lovingly created in half an hour.

Of bread bakers, Paul's the best.
He really is the master.
Just watching him mixing ingredients,
makes my heart beat faster.

It's no secret that Paul has a following.
He's referred to as the Silver Fox.
The only improvement to his bread...
...is if he makes some to serve with chocs.

I'm sure this TV programme will be popular.
You know, it's really no surprise,
that lots of us baking fans,
are smitten by Paul's smiley bright blue eyes.

So BBC2 keep up the good work.
It's really all jolly good,
bread baking and a sex symbol.
Thanks for Paul Hollywood!

79   Mum's crush

When I was a little girl my Mum used to say,
that if I didn't behave or be good as good as I can.
Then she'd be gone – run off one day.
Run off with a handsome man.

Now, I don't know if you can say these things today.
I'm not sure that it's P.C.
But, I worried about it and fretted,
that she'd run off and leave my Dad and me.

So. I'd be on my best behaviour,
be a good girl eating all my dinners and my teas,
and wash my hands and face,
and remember to say Thank You and Please.

I kept my bedroom tidy.
I put away all my toys.
I played quiet little girly games,
 and never made any noise.

And then one day I noticed it...
A photograph had appeared!
On her bedside table – a handsome man!
I just stared and stared.

Had Mum gone stark raving bonkers?
Had she gone totally mad,
to display a photo of her amour,
next to the bed she shared with Dad?

"Is this the man you are running off with?"
She laughed, "I don't think that I'll get far,
for he is a handsome man,
but, he's an unattainable film star".

I sighed with relief – it was true,
my Mum wasn't really running away.
Now, I have fond memories of her,
and remember when Harry Belafonte's picture came to stay!

80   My Dad

I had a happy childhood. Well...at least I think I had.
It was in the fifties and sixties, when I had you for my Dad.

You tried to keep me as your little girl,
although I aspired to be a tomboy.
Boys seemed to have more fun than girls,
doing rough stuff that I'd enjoy.

I discovered my brother's go cart,
that you had hidden in the shed, one day.
I only had one ride in it ...
...before you gave it away.

You told me it was dangerous. "Not for girls!" you said.
I might fall out and hurt myself...I might just end up dead!

I wanted to learn to whistle. You stopped me and said again,
"A whistling woman and a crowing hen,
is neither good for God or men".

Every time I wanted to try something new,
you'd speak to me in a voice calm and tender.
But with hindsight I realise that you steered me away,
from things not deemed suitable for my gender.

So...I never got to play football,
at cricket never had a go.
You encouraged mum to teach me to knit,
and when that failed ...encouraged me to sew.

In the sixties...girls were girls,
and boys were definitely boys.
I must have irritated you by not conforming.
not having female skills or ploys.

I wanted a Meccano set for Christmas,
but, you said it was just for boys.
So I was really surprised and amazed,
to find a set with my Christmas toys.

Maybe you saw my potential.
Or maybe you finally got 'me'.
But you gave me a chance to be different,
and to try my hand at technology.

It was different in the sixties.
Back in those days of old.
So thanks Dad for allowing me to express myself,
and break out of that expected female mould.

81   My Dad 2

You were a gentle giant. Mostly happy... hardly ever sad.
You were a loving father. You ...were my Dad.

I have happy memories of you.
You spent lots of quality time with me.
We were always on adventures.
Especially to places that were free.

The Arboretum was a favourite.
Listening to brass bands in the park.
Eating sugar butties and drinking cold tea.
We always had a great lark.

One of my favourite memories. The one that I really like,
is of a trip to Bluebell Woods, having a croggy on your bike.

We used to go to the cemetery, to visit your first wife's grave.
Bribing me with ice cream, this secret to share and save.

But...Mum always knew.
And would ask me where we had been.
And with the innocence of a child...
I would tell her and have to come clean.

I remember the time when you lost me.
It was at Nottingham Goose Fair.
I was safely in the lost children's tent,
magic painting in a book of Rupert Bear.

Again you bribed me with a present.
An expensive doll that was such a cost.
And when mum asked why you had bought it.
I told her it was because I had been lost.

I must have been a liability, I could never keep Schtum,
every time that we messed up...well... I just had to tell mum.

I hope you never got into trouble.
I know that you always meant for the best...
It was just unfortunate that....
...you had a daughter who was such a pest.

So...Dad...you've left me with many memories.
So many thoughts to ponder on...
And when I wonder about you...
I see you mirrored in my lovely son.

Another lovely father.
Making memories for his daughter and son.
Continuing the Garside tradition
passing on what you had begun.

I love you Thomas Garside. You were a fantastic Dad.
And my son...who never met you...is another fantastic lad.

It's odd how thing go in cycles,
something in the genes I've guessed.
But I see you, Dad, living in my son
and I feel so really blessed...

Birthdays and Celebrations

I can't always find the right birthday card, with the words that I want to convey, so I have been having a go at writing my own.

One of my favourite poetry books Is Christmas by UA Fanthorpe. I am trying to emulate her by attempting to write a Christmas poem each year to send as an email message.

"Christmas in Bulwell Village" was written as a song, that I performed at a friend's Boxing Day party. Votes were placed for whose party piece was the best. I lost to a friend who played his guitar behind his head. I was robbed!

Quote from a birthday card

"These birthday wishes are sent especially for you
May love and happiness be all around and may all your wishes
come true".

Which wishes are these then?
The wish where I long to be tall and slender.
Or the wish for a fully fitted kitchen,
with new appliances and blender?

I crossed my fingers and made my wish.
Closed my eyes real tight.
I wished and wished and wished,
and wished with all my might
I wished that I'd be lithe and slim,
graceful, slender and tall.
But when I opened up my eyes,
my wish hadn't been answered at all.

Or maybe the wish is the one,
where I can eat chocolate all day and every night,
and still keep a good complexion and a figure lithe and slight?

Or possibly it's the wish for a shorter working day,
10 till 3 with a 4 hour lunch - now that would be O.K!

Or perhaps these wishes are for instant wealth,
celebrity and fame.
My poems read throughout the world,
 and my name a household name?

So, what do I wish? Cos they never ever work!
I've never had one come true.
I'll just stick with the love and happiness,
that's what I usually do.

83   Christmas Message

Here's my annual message.
A yearly way to stay in touch.
Despite not seeing you often,
I think of you so much.

It appears to be at Christmastime,
that there seems to be a special reason,
to wish you all the very best,
and the compliments of the season.

So, here's the message for you.
Even though we are many miles apart.
I wish you all the best for you and yours,
from the bottom, and the top, of my heart.

As another year goes whizzing by,
I wish you whatever you wish for yourself.
And as we all get older (and wiser),
I wish for you - lots of good health!

It's Christmas in Bulwell village,
and I met Santa Claus.
He made a special delivery to my house.
Did he visit yours?
He said I was a good girl,
and I was on the list labelled nice.
Sure enough, at the top of the list,
I read my name Joy Rice.

It's Christmas in Bulwell village,
Listen to St Mary's bells ring.
People dancing in the streets.
Children sweetly sing.

It's Christmas in Bulwell village,
and I met a snowman chap.
He lived on Durham Crescent
and he wore a festive flat cap.
He said he loved the village
and you know he can't be wrong.
So join with me this Christmas time
and sing the Bulwell village song

It's Christmas in Bulwell village,
Listen to St Mary's bells ring.
People dancing in the streets.
Children sweetly sing.

It's Christmas in Bulwell village
and I met a Christmas elf
He was off to Poundland
to see what bargains were on the shelf.
He said that Bulwell village
had all the best quality stores.
Tesco's, Wilko's and B & N
who could ask for anything more.

85   <u>Christmas past</u>

The Satsumas have all wizened up.
The last chocolate brazil has been ate.
The remaining brussels have gone mouldy,
the chestnuts are past their sell by date.

The turkey has all been gobbled up,
so has the roast pork and boiled ham too.
All that's left is uncrackable walnuts,
and then...there is only a few!

The mince pies have all been devoured.
The Christmas cake vanished into thin air.
It was in the pantry before Christmas,
and disappeared by the start of the new year.

There's no Thornton's continentals left in this house.
No Terry's chocolate orange, nor any selection box.
The fancy shortbread has all been eaten,
so have the Toblerone and all of the chocs.

The Radio Times is redundant,
full of programmes that I never got 'round to view.
There was always something to be eaten,
plus too many other things to do.

Time to put away the Christmas C.D.s
no more listening to Nat or to Bing.
Nor more Aled, walking in the air with snowmen,
no more heralding angels that sing.

The walls where the Christmas cards were festooned,
bear the remnants of unmoveable blu-tak.
The decorations have all fallen down,
the balloons are all shrivelled and slack.

I shall be vacuuming up pine needles for ages,
and finding strands of tinsel for weeks.
I can see that this grand new year clean-up,
has got me practising my cleaning techniques.

The holly has all gone manky.
All that's left of the candles - a waxy mess.
I think that I am suffering a new illness,
post - Christmas - clearing -up -stress!

But I'm getting ready for next time.
I've made a list - nearly as long as two yards,
and although it's only January...
...I've already bought wrapping paper and cards!

86   If you counted friendship in pounds and pence

If you counted friendship in pounds and pence,
it really would be true!
That I'd be a lottery winner,
with a valuable friend like you.

87   Let's put Christ back into Christmas!

Let's put Christ back into Christmas!
Despite what the PC brigade say,
remember that Jesus' birth is the true reason
that we celebrate Christmas Day!

Bring out the dusty manger scene,
make it central to your feast.
Put it in a place of honour,
for baby Jesus - the Prince of Peace.

Bring out your stored away Christmas tree,
display it with great pride!
Forget about any pagan connotations,
think about the 'tree' on which He died.

Set out the figures in your Nativity set
to remind you of the Christmas story,
shepherds, kings, the holy family
and angels singing of God's Glory.

Don't worry about offending other religions.
They too have their own special days.
Christmas belongs to us Christians,
so, let's celebrate and praise!

Don't hide your Christmas lights under a bushel.
Stick 'em up and let 'em shine out bright,
in remembrance of a special star
on that very first Christmas night.

Enjoy this Christmas season,
despite the snow and freezes.
May you feel the warmth of this special time
and share in the love of Jesus!

As Lennon and McCartney wrote,
"Love is all you need".
So, remember Love this Christmas,
in a world that seems mad with greed.

Ponder on the poverty,
of that simple stable scene.
Why did God choose that poor place?
What does it really mean?

For in the shepherds, angels, kings.
Characters of the Nativity crèche.
Central to it all is - Jesus the Christ,
God's word - Love - made flesh.

The angels sang their hearts out,
Hallelujah and Glory from above.
The message sent from heaven to earth,
All you need is love!

So, spread some love this Christmas time.
Share a smile, a kind word, a good deed.
Give time to others, show you care.
Love is all you need!

Marriage is like a garden,
it needs good management and care.
It pays to keep on top of things,
and it's easier when you both share.

When planning your garden, or marriage,
first consider the over-all grand design.
Nurture it like a tender spring seedling.
Nourish with love, kisses and sunshine.

Keep your marriage in perfect condition.
Tend it constantly - don't leave things to chance.
For, like a garden that's best in the summer,
may your lives be filled with flowers, fragrance and romance.

Show off your marriage with pleasure,
let it be your delight and great pride.
And, as it flourishes through each passing year,
remember the day when you were a new groom and bride.

May your lives be full and fragrant,
full of sweet-scented blossom perfume.
May your lives together be all that you hope for.
May your marriage flourish and bloom.

So - a toast for your wedding and the future.
All the best for all the many years to come.
Enjoy your time spent together,
marriage, like gardening, should be fun!

First, select your happy home,
add lashings of love and care.
Put in some fun and laughter,
and happy times to share.

Take two armfuls of cuddles,
or better still - use caresses.
Mix in a never ending supply of hugs,
blend to get rid of life's stresses.

Pour in plenty of patience.
Stir in lots of kisses.
Season with a sense of humour,
whisk with realistic wishes.

Infuse with a dash of tolerance,
and a dollop of concern and caring.
Sprinkle in some tenderness,
and quality time for sharing.

Marinade all ingredients together.
Be careful not to ruin!
Tenderise with love galore,
and continue with the wooing!

Simmer for a lifetime.
Stir well to keep from clogging.
Spice things up with 'you know what'
and season well with snogging!

Thank you for being my friend.
I really think it's great,
that you have always been for me,
a truly special mate!

We might have been friends for a lifetime,
or maybe just a few years.
But you have been there for me,
through the smiles and the tears.

I really am so grateful,
that you have been my friend,
a person I can share with,
someone on whom I can depend.

Sometimes, we might not see each other.
But always try to keep in touch.
It makes me appreciate the times,
we do meet up, really so very much.

You friendship has been a big influence.
I think that you can see,
that knowing you has played a part,
in making the person that is me.

So, Thank you for your friendship.
I'm really a lucky gal!
I thank the Lord for choosing you
to be my special pal!

Cats

I love cats!

92   <u>Emerald</u>

It is with thanks and gratitude that,
I say Thank You for Emerald, my own dear cat.
It is a precious blessing of mine,
to be honoured by this friendship so feline.

For a cat can be a fussy pussy and will pick and choose,
the human that she favours with her mews.
So, you see Em and me we're more than owner and pet,
we are two of a kind; we are part of a set.

Stroking a cat (it's been proven) is a calming therapy,
and it really is soothing having a cat sat on your knee.
But, I can't work it out. No, I really can't see.
Who benefits the most? Is it Emerald? Or me?

A cat adds something to a house,
sometimes a dead sparrow...or a half chewed mouse.
It's a gift from her - a little present to me,
her way of saying thanks for bed & board for free.

So, Thanks be for puss, for cats and kittens too,
for all furry creatures that purr and mew.
You may think that I'm daft or even soggy,
but I really am grateful for my own dear moggy.

For the love of Emerald is its own reward,
and with a grateful heart, I say Thank you, Lord!

If our love could have saved you,
you'd still be with us, today.
But your life was complete; your time was up,
and so you slipped away.

Our tears could not stop the process.
We knew that you were dying.
And even though we tried to be brave for you,
we couldn't keep from crying.

So, goodbye our beloved Em.
A friend, faithful and true.
Time for you to rest.
There's a special place in Heaven for you.

When you were younger, you'd greet me,
as I came home from work, each day.
Wanting food, fuss and friendship,
wanting to romp and play.

You'd greet me at the door,
all meowing and excited.
So wait for me at Heaven's door,
until the day we are reunited.

I'll look for friends and family,
who have gone on before.
But you're the one I want to greet me.
when I arrive at Heaven's door.

I'll pick you up and cuddle you,
and stroke your silky, soft fur.
But, best of all to look in your eyes
and hear your gentle purr.

I have a talking cat - she really is amazing!
Once, when locked out of my house...
                    ...I saw her through the double glazing.
She sat upon the sofa and underneath her paw,
I noticed that she had got the spare key to the front door.
"Let me in", I begged her, "open up right now".
My amazing talking cat looked me in the eye,
            and answered with ..."me, how?"

One day, whilst in the garden as the cat lay in the herbage,
I wondered to myself if she was feeling very verbage.
When thinning out the border, I saw a weed quite noxious,
and pussy sitting in the catnip looking quite precoxious.
"Please, would you be so kind," I asked
                    "and pass me the trowel?"
My cat yawned and vocalised the answer..."me, howl?"

Whilst watching TV with the cat sat on my knee.
I got a sudden urge to go and have...
                        ...a nice refreshing cup of tea.
Upon returning to my seat,
                    I found my cat beginning to growol,
as she sat watching Channel 4,
                    in charge of the remote control.
"Please pass that zapper to me", I gently asked my cat.
She looked me in the eye and said... "Now how can I do that?
I know that we are matey; I know that we are chums.
But, don't you realise that us cats...cannot talk ...
                    ...nor do we have opposable thumbs!"

Do you ever get fed up with your lot?
Do you feel that life is mundane?
Would life be better if I wasn't me,
but, instead could start over again?

If there is, can I choose?
Could I be this? Or maybe that?
For if there's any opportunity for choosing,
then I would really like to be a cat!

Because, cats don't have to pay mortgages
or worry about unpaid bills.
Cats doss around all day sleeping,
on your best armchairs or windowsills.

You don't see many cats in the workplace,
or ever find them waiting in a dole queue.
Cats are usually hanging around the garden,
often too tired even to mew.

Cats don't have to do the shopping,
lugging carrier bags from Sainsbury's to the house.
Cats get biscuits plus two meals a day,
supplemented by the occasional mouse.

Cats can sleep for 18 hours out of 24,
they could fall asleep on a clothes line.
I've never met a cat that had insomnia,
they just never seem to have the time.

Cats have a superior outlook.
it's because they were once worshipped as gods,
and cats still think 'no change there then,'
the arrogant little sods!

Cats get lots of affection from their owners,
with strokings and ticklings of their fur.
You can estimate the depth of their contentment,
by the loud volume of their purr.

Is there such a thing as reincarnation?
Is there an afterlife?
Do we get the option to return?
To have another chance of life?

For you can see why I'd wish to be a cat,
to be looked after and have no cares would be oh so nice.
And to sleep all day and go out on the tiles each night,
well... that would be my idea of paradise!

There are no cats in the bible.
Now isn't that absurd,
that of God's greatest creation,
there's no mention ...not a word!

There are all kinds of animals mentioned.
Camels, lions, goats and especially sheep.
But what of the finest feline?
...Well, nothing...not a peep!

Now, in the Garden of Eden.
When animal's names were handed out.
Surely, Adam must have named the moggy?
Puss, Tabby, Kitty - you could hear him shout.

What about on Noah's Ark?
When all the animals came in two by two?
Surely there were cats on board?
For cats don't like water - it's true.

And, when Moses visited Pharaoh.
Well you really would have thought,
that there would be cats aplenty,
for they were Gods in Pharaoh s court.

And all throughout the stories.
No signs of cat or kit.
I wonder if they just weren't there?
Or maybe their furry faces didn't fit?

No parables of the Prodigal Puss.
No musings on the Missing Mog.
Guess cats just weren't popular,
overshadowed by the dog?

But, though I love the Bible,
and I love moggies too.
I really would enjoy it more,
if I could combine the two.

I know that Jesus loved everyone.
He was such an awesome chap.
That I would love to see an image of him,
stroking a cat balanced in his lap.

Christian Women's Fellowship

For many years I have been actively involved in the Christian Women's Fellowship.

Firstly, as someone that attended, then over the years joining in more and also performing my poems at the Saturday night concert at our annual weekend away.

For the past 6 years I have been their publicity officer promoting the weekend events. This has also led to the creation of an email prayer link – cwf197@gmail.com

For more details check out our blog
http://christianwomensfellowship.blogspot.co.uk

Part of my tasks on the weekend has been to say Grace at one of the meals. I have usually made something up.
Here are a couple that I remembered to write down.

Many poems written as a result of CWF and prayer requests are in the sections –
Religious stuff – Trying to be a good Christian,
Women's problems, Life, Birthdays and Celebrations

Bless our breakfast and bless us Lord,
as we sit here with one accord.

Thank you for our breakfast.
Thank you Lord for all of the choices.
As we sit and ponder our Authentic Lives,
and our Authentic Voices.

Thank you for the nourishment,
we have shared - to help our spirits revive.
Thanks you for our Authentic Choices,
and our Authentic Lives.

On this day as our conference ends.
Bless us Lord as we sit amongst good friends.
And, may we take home, memories of all we've done.
Faith, Food, Friendship, Fellowship and Fun!

98   Grace for Unconditional Love 2014

Come and join our breakfast!
There's food and love to share!
Everyone is welcome,
especially those who love teddy bears!

Now that the Christmas and New Year festivities are over,
and you feel in need of a pick me up tonic.
Why not consider joining your CWF friends, this February,
at The Hayes conference centre in Swanwick?

Winter months can be dark and dreary,
when all is said and done.
So consider joining with us,
for Friendship, Faith and Fun!

Our weekend has serious stuff like Bible study,
or maybe try creativity and crafts?
There's free time for chatting and catch-ups,
and also for sharing lots of laughs.

There are workshops on various topics,
time to sit with others and share.
Fairtrade, Justice, Hospitality – Important issues,
not forgetting time for a prayer!

Unconditional Love is our theme ,
our speakers – Street Angels will share about their outreach.
Unconditional Love is what we are about,
join us and let's practice what we preach.

100   Comforted = Comfort ted

My name is Teddy Gaga, I am a party ted.
I like to knock back the Baileys and get right off my head.

We're doing the latest craze – it's called Neknominate
But ooh-er... all those Baileys haven't left me feeling so great.

The street angels helped me;
 they showed me love and care.
They mopped me up, gave me a lollipop,
 and offered me a prayer!

I was struggling in my high heels and to the street I drops.
Thank goodness for their comfort and for their free flip flops.

My head was throbbing, my feet ached,
I was a very sore ted,
But thanks to the angels comforting me ,
I am now on my way to being sorted.

They gave me a holding cross and told me about our saviour.
Now I'm saved, too.
Cut down on the booze, no longer a little raver.

For more teddy poems plus the photos – look at our blog!
http://christianwomensfellowship.blogspot.co.uk

For more information on Christian Nightlife Initiatives – Street Angels
www.sa-CNI.org.uk

In 2007 Christian's Women's' Fellowship was 80 years old –
the same as our Queen, here is a poem that I sent to Her
Majesty.

101   Happy Birthday to our own dear Queen

Happy Birthday to our own dear Queen.
Our best wishes we want you to know.
We all think that you're great and we all love you,
As you celebrate the big Eight-O!

Your Majesty doesn't look, dress or act as if you are 80.
You've improved with age... like a fine wine.
If your next 80 years are as good as the first,
then I think that you'll be just fine!

Good luck Ma'am, on this birthday,
for reaching the sum of four score.
We all wish you the best for the future,
and wish that you'll have many more!

So raise your glasses let's make a toast,
Happy Birthday to Elizabeth R.
Long life, good luck and all things nice,
to our fantastic royal star!

Hip Hip Hooray!
Hurrah Whoopee!
Let's all celebrate,
our Queen's eighty!

Bonus Chapter – Ten extra poems!

102   <u>All of my bras have gone tight</u>

I try to be careful what I eat,
often choosing low-fat or lite.
So, why is it - that I've recently noticed,
that all of my bras have gone tight?

It's not because I've had a boob job,
I've never thought that I might.
But, something is expanding up there,
as all of my bras have gone tight!

Sometimes, in the morning when dressing,
putting my bra on turns into a fight.
I can't get my bazooms reined in properly,
now that all of my bras have gone tight.

They're all bulging and spilling over.
God knows I must look a sight!
Struggling to get them contained,
because all of my bras have gone tight.

This struggle could go on for ever,
I'm sure there must be others who share my plight...
....unless I'm the only one in England,
suffering because all of my bras have gone tight.

The only thing that is helpful,
truly a comfort, a joy and delight,
at the end of the day when that bra comes off.
Yes! That really is a good night!

103   Approaching fabulous

If it's true that we improve with age.
Then I must be approaching fabulous right now.
I've mellowed, matured and acquired a bloom.
I've acquired that female mystique know how.

I'm fully seasoned! I'm completely ripe!
I'm totally at my peak.
I'm at my best! Pick me now...
...As my sell by date is next week!

104   Best Friend

I asked God for a good friend...
And He gave me one of the best!
For, in having you as my friend,
I know that I am truly blest.

I asked God for a good friend...
And He introduced you to me.
For, in having you as my friend,
a kindred spirit you turned out to be.

So, Thank You, God for good friends!
They are like angels from above.
We are blessed to have them with us,
for their friendship, care and love.

I never thought when I asked God,
just who He might choose to send.
So, Thanks to God for choosing,
and send you to be my friend.

105   Bulwell Common

Whatever the season,
or time of year,
the wind on Bulwell Common,
will blow through your hair.

It doesn't matter,
which way you are facing.
The wind on Bulwell Common,
is Skegness bracing.

Bulwell Common! Bulwell Common!
The place that I hold dear.
The winds up there will blow your hat off!
And mess up all your hair!

Sometimes the wind is gentle.
Just a soft and gentle breeze,
but mostly it's a blooming gale,
that will bring you to your knees.

Sometimes it's a warm waft of air,
and you think hmm this is nice...
But mostly it's so freezing,
turning your ears to blocks of ice.

So if you want some fresh air,
Bulwell Common is the place to be.
Skegness air blows up there,
and the common is nearer than the sea!

106   I had a winter baby

I had a winter baby,
with hair like platinum snow.
My winter boy with eyes of sky blue,
born in a winter long ago.

I had a summer baby.
with hair like golden corn.
My summer boy with sunny smiles,
on a sunny day was born.

I had a springtime baby,
a girl with copper hair.
My springtime girl so full of fun,
with love enough to spare.

My winter, summer, spring children,
are all now grown and flown away.
Where have the seasons gone?
What happened to yesterday?

But although time is passing,
the days, weeks, months and years fly past.
I remember all of those far off happy times,
my memories sustain me and last.

But though children grow up and leave,
the best is yet to come...
Grandchildren arrive....what a delight!
Years and years of fun!

I'm really a positive person.
But sometimes I have my negative days.
People just don't see it my way;
they only see it their own ways.

I'm really an optimistic person.
But sometimes I'm a right pessimist.
Why are some people just false friends?
It really drives me round the twist.

I'm really a kind, loving person.
But sometimes others make me so mad.
Why do people not accept me as I am?
You know it really makes me feel so sad.

I'm trying to learn some life lessons.
I'm being true to myself...honest and caring.
I'm rising above these negative feelings,
and my positive vibes I am sharing!

I'm really a cheerful, happy person;
no longer will I let myself be stressed.
I'm loved by many - family and friends,
Thank God! For I know I am truly blessed!

<u>I love the Hokey Cokey</u>

I love the Hokey Cokey.
I love all the ins and outs.
I love the knee bends and rah rahs.
I love to shake it all about.

But...if what the Hokey Cokey
is really what it's all about?
What does that say about your Life?
Are you in or are you out?

It seems to me that you have to put in,
before you can take it out.
The more you put in, the more you get out,
of that there is no doubt.

When you are feeling sad and lonely,
why not go out for a walkabout?
Smile at others, say, "Hello",
and you'll feel your life turnabout.

When you have anger welling up,
go outside and scream and shout.
Get the anger outside.
C'mon shake it all about!

When life seems to be crushing,
and everything seems inside out.
Why not say a little prayer?
It works you don't have to be devout.

So put plenty of zest into your life.
C'mon have a big smile - don't pout.
Remember put plenty in - take little out.
And give it a damn good shake about.

109 Life is great!

Life is great!
Celebrate and love it!
If a problem comes your way,
then try to rise above it.

Life is great!
Rejoice and sing out loud.
Look for the silver lining,
in each and every cloud.

Life is great!
Let me explain...
...If you want a rainbow,
then first there must be rain.

Life is great!
You never know what to expect.
Life is full of surprises!
Treat life with respect!

<u>Poppies</u>

Did you get that email?
I think it's been around everywhere
...The one about planting poppies...
...I thought it was a great idea!

The plan is for us all to plant poppies,
in any waste land or open space.
To remind us of that terrible First World War,
all the lives lost ...all that waste.

If there is a bit of waste land near you,
a hedgerow or side of a field,
sprinkle some Poppy seeds there,
and a crimson crop they'll yield.

All of us will know of someone,
our granddads or our dads,
who fought and died for freedom,
and lots of them were only lads.

This year when it's the anniversary,
and our open spaces are blooming red,
pause and say a thank you for freedom,
and remember 'our glorious dead'.

Wars will always be with us,
an end to conflict is my prayer.
So, I'll plant and wear my Poppy,
to show that I remember...and I care.

111 <u>Since you've been gone</u>

Since you've been gone,
the house is too quiet.
There's a yawning silence,
instead of the usual riot.

No sound from the TV
No music blaring too.
No catch up TV on your computer,
as you've taken it with you.

No invading my personal space,
demanding, "What are we doing today?"
It's all gone quiet and boring,
since you went away.

No Orange Wednesdays,
no hitting the town.
No wonder I'm feeling,
so sad and down.

There's an ache in my chest,
that I can't explain.
An emptiness there...
...slowly filling with pain.

I can't watch reality TV,
without shedding a tear.
We should be laughing at it together,
but you're not here.

I stand at your wardrobe,
to catch a trace of your perfume.
I keep looking for you,
but there's just an empty room.

I'd known for a while,
that it was time for you to fly and leave the nest.
And, I was pleased to let you go,
despite this ache in my chest.

I bet you are laughing and joking,
and having a really great time.
And I can imagine you saying,
"Oh no, Mum, not another rhyme!"

---

111 poems plus 2 (prayer walk and some sad stuff).

Thank you for purchasing this book. These poems have been composed and written over several years. I hope that you enjoyed reading them as much as I enjoyed writing them.

God Bless

Joy

Check out my website – www.joyrice.co.uk

I also have a Facebook page – Joy's Poems - on which I try to put a poem or verse a day.

Need a performance poet or speaker for your group?

Contact – joyricepoet@gmail.com